LIFE IS TOUGH BUT

 IS

FAITHFUL

LIFE IS TOUGH BUT

God IS
FAITHFUL

How to See God's Love
in Difficult Times

SHEILA WALSH

A
JANET
THOMA
BOOK

THOMAS NELSON PUBLISHERS
Nashville

Published in Nashville, Tennessee, by Thomas Nelson, Inc.

Life Is Tough but God Is Faithful combines new material with updated portions from the author's *Holding On to Heaven with Hell on Your Back* (1990) and *Sparks in the Dark* (1992).

Scripture quotations noted NKJV are from THE NEW KING JAMES VERSION. Copyright © 1979, 1980, 1982, 1990, Thomas Nelson, Inc.

Scripture quotations noted TLB are from *The Living Bible*, copyright © 1971. Used by permission of Tyndale House Publishers, Inc., Wheaton, Illinois 60189. All rights reserved.

Scripture quotations noted NCV are from the HOLY BIBLE: NEW CENTURY VERSION. Copyright © 1987, 1988, 1991 by Word Publishing. All rights reserved.

Scripture quotations noted NIV are from the HOLY BIBLE: NEW INTERNA-TIONAL VERSION®. Copyright © 1973, 1978, 1984 by International Bible Society. Used by permission of Zondervan Publishing House. All rights reserved.

Library of Congress Cataloging-in-Publication Data

Walsh, Sheila

Life is tough but God is faithful / Sheila Walsh.
p.   cm.
Includes bibliographical references.
ISBN 0-7852-6914-2 (hc)
ISBN 0-7852-6672-0 (pb)
1. Christian life. 2. Walsh, Sheila, 1956–   . I. Title.
BV4501.2.M494 1999
248.4—dc21   99-10924
                                                                          CIP

Printed in the United States of America

16 17 18 PHX 07 06 05 04

DEDICATION

This book is dedicated to my darling son, Christian. It's my prayer, little lamb, that as you grow into a young man, you will know the faithfulness of God in the dark days and in the best days of your life. Your daddy and I love you, sweet boy.

CONTENTS

Acknowledgments

I am deeply grateful to Janet Thoma. We have walked many miles together, and I love your heart, your talent, and your vision. You are a true friend.

1

THE WHOLE POINT

===

It's the message in a hymn I remember from my childhood: "Nothing in my hands I bring; simply to Thy cross I cling."

William and Eleanor Pfaehler, the parents of my husband, Barry, have become my American family. How blessed I am to have families from two of the best countries in the world, Scotland and America!

In the spring of 1998 my mother-in-law, who has liver cancer, called me from Charleston. "I'm frustrated because I'm not sure my own doctor is telling me the whole truth," Eleanor said. "I don't know if he is trying to protect me or he just doesn't know."

I heard the pain in her voice and wanted to do everything I could to help. "Why don't you come to Nashville? One of the best cancer specialists in the country is at Baptist Hospital," I said. "I'll go with you and we will get a second opinion . . . Bring all your charts and everything you have."

Eleanor ended our phone conversation that day by saying, "I know I won't go one day after—or one day before—the time God has allotted for me."

Barry's dad and mother flew into Nashville the next month and stayed with us for a month. William was finding it hard to face the fact that his wife is dying, that he is losing his best friend for the last forty-seven years. He didn't really want to know everything the doctor had to say; it's a very painful thing for him. But because Barry's mom is the kind of person who wants to know exactly what medical science says, she wanted to know the truth. Then she would make peace with that.

William, or Bubsie as we fondly refer to him, didn't want to come, so Barry and I drove down to the doctor's with her. As we were driving I said, "Tell me, how do you want this to go? Do you want him to just lay it on the line?"

"Absolutely. I want to know everything he can tell me."

We sat in the waiting room. We were all kind of quiet. I looked up on the wall and saw these words:

WHAT CANCER CAN'T DO

Can't steal your memories.
Can't rob your joy.
Can't touch your eternity.
Can't remove you from God's care.
Can't stop you from loving and being loved.

"Did you see that?" I asked Eleanor. No, she hadn't. So I read it to her. As she heard the words, tears began running down her face. "I know that's true, but it is good to hear it again."

Later, when the doctor came into the consultation room, I said, "My mother-in-law is here. She knows she has liver cancer, and she would like to know exactly what her prognosis is."

"Let me make one thing clear," he said. "I'm a doctor. I'm one of the nation's leading cancer specialists, but I am also a Christian. I know that what I tell you is from the best of my experience, but I also know that your days are in God's hands and they are marked down in His book."

The doctor went through all of the charts and then said, "Okay. The bottom line is you have anywhere from six months to two years. You are not on any kind of chemo. You have had fifty shots, and there is a new kind of treatment we can give you as a final last lap. You need to wait until there are some physical signs. Your skin will turn yellow, you will get pain in your left shoulder, and your liver will enlarge."

Mom asked, "What will this regimen do for me?"

"All it will do is buy you a little more time."

"How sick will I be?"

The doctor admitted that she would be pretty sick.

Eleanor thought only for a moment. Then she replied, "I will opt not to do that."

"I respect that," he answered, but we could see a quizzical look in his eyes so she explained.

"The reason is, I have a grandson." Then she started to cry. "My biggest fear is that he won't remember me. I want to be able to enjoy him and spend time with him every day I have left."

Life is tough. My mother-in-law is not alone. Most of us struggle with difficult challenges throughout our lives. Over the last two years more than a half million women have attended Women of Faith conferences. Face to face or in letters they ask me . . .

- "If God loves me, why did my child die?"
- "If God hears my prayers, why am I still single?"
- "If God is in control of the world, why is life so hard?"

A little wrong information is worse than no information at all. I think it's easier to reach a completely unchurched person with the message of the grace and love of God than to reach someone who has grown up in the church community but missed the point. We think we know the song, and we think we've heard the story. So we close our ears to the overwhelming news of the ridiculously lavish love of God, just as did a young student who wrote to me after one conference. I'll call her Susan.

> I was raised in church, so I have heard of Jesus and His love ever since I was a baby. My mother and father thought I was the perfect Christian teenager. When I left for college, they were sure I'd be able to stand my ground. So was I. But I failed in every situation possible. I felt like the lowest life on earth. I just knew that I could never be forgiven.

Susan went on to talk about her recent attendance at a Women of Faith conference:

I remember sitting in my chair surrounded by thousands of Christian women singing and laughing. But I could not join in. I was dying inside. When you spoke you opened a part of my heart that had been hardened for so long. As I sat there crying I rededicated my life to God. I returned to school with a new outlook and a lot of books. I felt rejuvenated for about a week, then all the old guilt and shame came back. I had already failed and I could not change.

THE SAME OLD STORY

Susan's letter could have been written by almost any of us who have missed God's punch line. I relate to her fervent commitment to be able to stand at college and make God and family proud of her. The truth is, ultimately none of us will be able to stand unless we daily throw ourselves into the saving arms of God. We can't do it on our own. It's not about us. We have no strength apart from Him.

It took me almost forty years to truly "get it." I realized this one night when I was telling Barry about a friend who had totally missed the point of a joke I'd told her.

Then I thought, *But that's what I did for almost forty years. Totally missed the point.* Totally missed the heart of the gospel. Missed the message of God's faithfulness and love. I was blind to the finished work of Christ. I read the Bible over and over and then asked the same dumb internal questions:

- "How can I make God love me more?"

- "What do I need to do to be worthy of God's love?"

- "What makes God answer some people's prayers and not others?"

- "Why do I feel so far away from God?"

I missed the whole point. It's the message in a hymn I remember from my childhood: "Nothing in my hands I bring; simply to Thy cross I cling."

That hymn cries out, "It's all been done!"

Yet we're still working so hard to make God love us, and if life is tough we wonder what we've done wrong. So much human love is based on performance. If you're thin enough (or smart enough or pretty enough or . . .) you will be loved. We paste this on the heart of God and think that's how He is. Our battered egos want to believe that something about us can earn or lose the love of God. Nothing about us can do this.

When Susan left the conference and headed back to school, she had a fresh determination to do better. I understand that. We listen to a message that moves us or we read a book that touches us deep in our souls, and we are caught up again in a fresh cycle of "I blew it last time but this time it'll be different."

The problem with that is, Susan took Susan back to school. That's life! We take ourselves wherever we go. If it were as simple as understanding that God is worth a life lived well, there would be no need for Calvary. If we had the capacity to do better next time, then Christ's blood would not have been spilled.

We are right to want to do better. God is worth that—and much more. But the harsh reality of life this side of Eden is that we are powerless to do so without the faithfulness and love of God.

Ask the psalmist David. He loved God and committed adultery. He loved God and was responsible for sending a man to certain death. Look at Abraham. Father of his people—and also a liar. He allowed another man to sleep with his wife, saying that his wife was actually his sister. Thanks a lot, Abraham!

Look at Peter. Privileged to walk side by side with Jesus day after day. Saw the miracles. Saw Lazarus raised from the dead. It's what we all long for. But when hard confrontation came, he said he'd never met Jesus.

Human history is an ongoing story of stumbling men and women and the constant grace and mercy of God. God hits straight shots with crooked arrows. It's all about Him, never about us, never about the quality of the arrow. But we forget this.

DOES SATAN SEEM TO BE WINNING?

Life is tough but God is faithful has become my motto. The Bible is full of stories of men and women who in the midst of the toughest situations of life discovered the faithfulness of God. Take just one man. Job.

The book of Job has always fascinated me. I've heard innumerable sermons on it and have read wonderful books about it, but every time I dig my shovel in, there is always fresh soil.

As Job's familiar story opens, we learn that he was a good man, a loyal husband, a caring father. He was also a friend of God.

Then the scene shifts to the courts of heaven. We see the angels coming before God, and Satan is among them.

God called Satan's attention to His servant Job. "No one else on earth is like him," said the Lord. "He is an honest man and innocent of any wrong. He honors God and stays away from evil" (Job 1:8).

But Satan wasn't impressed. "Of course, he's a good man. He's no fool. He loves You because it pays to love You. Take away all his fringe benefits, and You've lost Yourself one very selfish human being" (vv. 10–11).

But God didn't agree. He said, "You're wrong. Job is a friend of Mine. Even if he lost everything, he'd still love Me" (v. 12). In a sense, God staked His reputation on the life of one man. Sometimes I wonder if God doesn't do that with each of us. Don't we all go through moments when God allows Satan to see if we really are God's person?

God gave Satan permission to tear Job's life apart. He lost everything. His sons, daughters, and servants were killed and his vast herds of livestock stolen. Tragedy visited Job on every level.

LIGHT THROUGH BROKEN WINDOWS

Job left a light on for you and me. David's brokenness lit a candle in the dark. Peter's bruises gave me courage to walk on. This is the purpose of our lives. To learn to love God and to love one another. To let the light of Christ shine through the dark moments as well as in the glory days when everything is wonderful.

When Eleanor, Barry, and I left the doctor's office that

day in May I asked her, "Instead of going home, would you like to go for a cup of coffee?"

As we sat in the restaurant we began to talk. She said, "He didn't really tell me anything I didn't know. But it was wonderful to hear it from someone who believes as I do. When my earthly life is over, my other life is just beginning."

I touched her hand and looked squarely into her eyes. "Your biggest fear is that people won't remember you. I wonder if you want to do something?

"Suppose we sit down in a room, just you and me—not Barry's dad, not Barry, not Christian. I will get out the video recorder and we'll talk.

"I want you to tell Christian how you met your husband—his granddad, how you felt when you were married, and how it felt when you were expecting Christian's dad.

"Then talk about the joy you felt when you found out you were to become a grandmother. Your first impressions of Christian. I want you to be able to leave a legacy, not just in words, but so he can look into your face and hear you tell him how much you love him."

That's a project we did Christmas week of 1998. Eleanor is dying, but God is faithful.

I know I couldn't do what I do without my mother and father-in-law.

William and Eleanor Pfaehler celebrated their forty-eighth wedding anniversary in 1998. Because of the special gift they are to Barry and me, I decided to surprise them one Friday night of the Women of Faith Conference in San Antonio. The first night of the conference I always take Christian on the stage for just a few minutes.

That night I decided I would also bring Barry's mom and dad on stage. I ordered a big bouquet of roses for Barry's mom. Usually his mom and dad stay backstage, but that evening I asked them to do me a special favor and sit out front, right in the front row.

When I came to the part where I normally bring Christian up, I said, "I want you to know I could not do what I do if it weren't for my mother- and father-in-law. They have traveled with us twenty-nine weekends this year.

"My mother-in law has liver cancer and my father-in-law has had two knee replacements that were not successful. He is in tremendous pain. Yet he stands behind the book table and sells books with Barry and talks with women. So many of the letters I get have a P.S.—say hi to your father-in-law. He makes so many friends. People love Bubsie!

"Barry's mother takes care of Christian when I'm speaking or doing a sound check or rehearsing, so I know if Christian is not with me, he is with his nana."

Then I brought my in-laws up on stage. I gave Eleanor the flowers.

I turned to Barry's dad. "I thought long and hard, Papa, about what I could give you. Then I realized I had already done it."

I turned and brought Christian up. I gave him to Barry's dad and William wept. By now the women at the conference were standing and clapping, many with tears in their eyes.

Life is tough but God is faithful. No one can rob you of your memories, your joy, your eternity, or can stop you from loving and being loved, as that sign in the doctor's office says.

Barry's dad knows that. Before I got pregnant, Bubsie

was having real trouble with his knees. (He will be eighty on his next birthday.) He asked his doctors about the possibility of knee replacement surgery, and they said it was a risky thing at his age but if it was successful it would make a significant difference in his life.

So he decided to have both knees replaced, even though he had never spent a day in the hospital before that time. We prayed for him, but the operation was not a success. He ended up with less mobility and more pain.

In the weeks after the surgery I watched him deteriorate before my eyes. He has always been an outgoing man, but he lost that zest for living. Now he didn't go out anymore. He used to be a very keen gardener. Now he sat around the house and said, "I'm in too much pain to move."

Then in the midst of that, Christian was born. The immediate change was almost like a miracle to me. He was up and out and constantly wanting to help with the baby. Bubsie had never been in more pain in his life, but recently he said to me, "Can you believe God saved the best days of my life for the end?"

Before Christmas of 1998 I bought Christian a big heavy slide. I watched Dad climb up and slide down with Christian. Later that day I watched him crawl around the floor, setting up a train set. Isn't that just like God? He does his physical therapy with a two-year-old! What a gift to my little boy. He is his papa's buddy for life.

LIFE IS TOUGH BUT GOD IS FAITHFUL

And remember Susan? There was more to her letter. After months of self-loathing and shame, she picked up one of the books she bought at the conference. It was *Honestly,* the story of my journey through clinical depression and hospitalization to true liberty in Christ. She wrote:

> I cannot tell you how it affected me. I felt the depression, shame, and guilt with you. And I saw you shine through. I knew I had hope and could be forgiven. I realize now that my life is not over. Because of Jesus' blood it has just begun.

Yes! Yes! Yes! That's it. Because of Jesus it's just begun. Life is tough but God is faithful.

In the following chapters, I talk about turning points to rediscovering God's love and faithfulness in tough times. When our dreams go sour or seem unfulfilled, we can choose to allow Satan to slither into our lives, or we can choose to remember that God is faithful, no matter how hopeless life gets. I've faced those kinds of choices myself. I want to share a little bit of how I went through my own kind of disillusionment when the most important relationships in my life were torn from me or left hanging by a thread.

As the British writer Thomas Hardy put it, "If a way to be better there be, it lies in taking a full look at the worst."

I've learned to get through difficult times by identifying critical choices we all face when the worst is on our backs. In the coming chapters, we will look at each of these turning points and see how people with simple, but determined, faith have been able to live in the worst kinds of situations and hold on anyway, suffering the worst kind of pain but never letting go of God's faithfulness.

Are you weary? Are you frightened?
When you go to bed, do you leave the light on?
When the cold wind blows to disturb your peace
Do you lock the door so no one else can see?
Broken promises have left their mark on you.
In your unbelief, one thing you must hold on to.

When the road becomes too rough,
When you're ready to give up,
When you're crying out for love,
God is faithful.

When your peace cannot be found,
He will never let you down.
You have chosen solid ground.
God is faithful.[1]

I believe that with all my heart. As I look back down the path of my life, I see the care God took every step of the way to draw me to His side. He spoke softly through all my years of trying to impress Him, "I love you. I will walk beside you. You can count on me."

I can't imagine the pain of losing all your children, your home, your health. I would never choose Job's life, and yet there is something about pain that repaints the picture of life. Of who we are, of who God is. I've said it myself. I look at my life. I think of the death of my father. I think of my struggle with clinical depression and that bleak winter of my soul, but even though I would not have chosen this path, I would not change a single day, a single step.

Why? Because I am a different woman. It's one thing to

say that the Lord is my shepherd; it's quite something else to be unable to walk one more step by yourself, to lean on that staff, and to be held up. It's just as Job said, "My ears had heard of you before, but now my eyes have seen you" (Job 42:5 NCV).

I've heard the same thing expressed by so many of you who share devastating losses but wouldn't go back because what you have tasted of the love and grace of God in the midst of pain is breathtaking. It's true!

Life is tough but God is faithful.
Life is tough but God is faithful.
Life is tough but God is faithful.

2

IT WASN'T SUPPOSED
TO BE THIS WAY

═══

When life doesn't make sense anymore, we can give up or we can remember who Jesus really is and that no matter how dark it gets, He is worth it all.

One day in 1989 a man of about sixty years of age called the *700 Club* to ask for help. I could tell that he was embarrassed and anxious about turning to a young woman for advice, but something made him call.

"I watched your program yesterday," he said. "You seem to care about people. I'm really sorry to take up your time, but I'm so unhappy."

I tried to reassure him that I was happy to talk with him and that I was a friend.

He told me that he'd been married for thirty-six years and now he'd ruined it all. I sat quietly praying for wisdom and let him continue.

"You see, I really love my wife, but years ago I had a

15

fling, nothing much, really, just a stupid fling. It lasted only a few weeks." As he continued his story, I could feel the anguish in his voice. He stopped for a moment.

"Does your wife know about this?" I asked.

"Well, you see, that's just it," he said. "I gave my life to God a few weeks ago, and I wanted to put things right. So I told my wife and asked her to forgive me, and now she's gone. She's gone." He began to cry bitterly, and I wished I could reach across the telephone miles and comfort him.

"It wasn't supposed to be this way," he said.

I heard those words everywhere I went.

The next day I interviewed Darrell Gilyard on *Heart to Heart*, my show that followed the *700 Club*. There was a buzz around CBN about my guest. I'd been told by several people who had seen him on Jerry Falwell's program that he was an unusual man of God. I knew very little about him as he took his seat beside me on the *Heart to Heart* set, but his story left an indelible mark on my heart.

When he was nine months old, his mother and father stood on the steps of a total stranger's home and gave their son away. This young black couple begged the older black woman who answered the door to care for their child for just a little while, but they never came back. So Darrell was raised by a godly, caring woman, who daily taught him about Jesus.

When he was just seven years old, she called him to her bedside. "Son, I'm dying. I'm poorer than your parents were, so I've nothing much to leave you." With that she thrust her old *Good News for Modern Man* Bible into his hands and said, "I leave you Jesus."

Darrell was passed from foster home to foster home. He was longing for love, trying to hold onto his faith.

When he was fourteen years old, he found himself out on the streets. He had no name, no family he knew, no one who cared if he lived or died. He made his bed under a bridge, selling cans and bottles to make enough to eat. He kept going to school, washing his one set of clothes in the river. At night he would sit under the light of a convenience store to do his homework. He was determined not to be a loser.

But there were plenty of cold nights when he lifted his face to the sky and asked God why. Was it too much to ask for a bed? For a friend? For someone to say goodnight to? As he stood there, a solitary figure against the night, he knew it wasn't supposed to be this way.

It wasn't supposed to be this way for Job either.

JOB'S PREDICAMENT

The Lord gave Satan permission to tear Job's life apart. But true to God's prediction, Job stood fast. In the midst of his sorrow, he declared, "The LORD gave and the LORD has taken away. Blessed be the name of the LORD" (Job 1:21 NKJV).

Not long afterward, God and Satan met again, and the Lord said, "Well, what do you think about Job now? Didn't I tell you there was nobody on earth like him? He was ruined for no reason, but he only praised My Name and continues to be without blame."

Satan sneered and retorted with a proverb often used by tradesmen of Job's time: "One skin for another! Of course, Job was willing to give up the lives of his animals, his servants, and his children, *but what about his own skin?* Every human is selfish. Why don't you let me touch Job's body and ruin his health? A man can live without his children. A man can live without his wealth, but cause him personal pain, and he'll curse You to Your face!"

"All right then," God replied. "Touch Job's body, but you cannot kill him."

And so Satan afflicted Job from the top of his head to the bottom of his feet with the most painful kinds of boils and sores. In incredible misery, Job sat on a heap of ashes, scraping his sores with a piece of broken pottery, but he never said a word against God.

What does Job's story have to say to you and me? Is it a dangerous thing to fall into the hands of God? Can He be trusted? What does it really mean to be His servant and His child? Why would God stand back and allow our mortal enemy to toy with us?

I've often wondered how Job prayed during those seven days and seven nights when the sky was like brass and nobody seemed to be listening. I wonder whether Job might at least have been tempted to mutter, *Lord, it wasn't supposed to be this way.*

No, a lot of life wasn't supposed to be this way, but it is. And when our prayers bounce off the ceiling and land right back in our faces, we feel guilty for asking why. After all, Christians are supposed to have all the answers. Theoretically, we are the ones who can deal with life because we have a powerful and loving God who hears our prayers and gives the victory. In reality, God often seems to respond with a "No," or a "Please wait. My plan is in place; just trust Me."

I believe that when we base our faith on apparent answered prayer, getting the solutions to our problems *right now*, we're in real trouble. If we mistake God's silence for indifference, we are the most miserable of people. If we give up when we no longer understand, we reject His caring, steadfast love and cut ourselves off from our only real hope.

Satan, of course, is sitting back hoping that that's exactly what will happen—that we will give up, quit, and pack it in. That's why Satan slithered up to a sixty-year-old heartbroken man whose wife had just left him after he tried to be honest. Satan said to him, "You were better off before you met God. You still had your wife then."

And that's why Satan crawled under the bridge to tell a lonely young boy, "You're forgotten. You're nobody. Why don't you end it all?"

Satan specializes in lies, confusion, desperation, and depression. As a fallen angel, he is a limited being, but he still has tremendous powers and the most clever strategies. He moves in to tempt us at our particular point of need, and he always times his temptations to come when we're feeling weak, stressed, desperate, and confused. He throws his worst in our faces and then sits back to see what will happen.

We often ask, "Can I really trust God? Where is He? Why isn't He riding to the rescue?" Perhaps the real question is, "Can God trust *me*?"

IS JESUS WORTH IT ALL?

If I say I'm willing to follow Jesus, what do I mean? I believe there is only one valid reason for following Jesus: because He is worth it. He is worth it—His love, His understanding, His compassion—because of who He is. I follow Him with no strings attached, not telling God that I'll do this if He'll come through with that. Either Jesus is worth it only because He is Jesus, or He is worth nothing.

━━━

Turning Point: When life doesn't make sense any-more, we can give up, or we can remember who Jesus really is and that, no matter how dark it gets, He is worth it all.

━━━

Those may seem like hard words to tell a teenager as he crawls into his cardboard box under the bridge to go to bed. I don't mean them as hard words, but as words of comfort. As he struggled to survive, all Darrell Gilyard had was Jesus.

As Darrell and I talked on *Heart to Heart* that morning, I looked into the eyes of this humble, gentle, strong man and realized that he understood a principle I had struggled with for years. He asked God one question—Why?—and then he was willing to wait for an answer. Days turned into weeks, which turned into months, and then years. Darrell kept wait-ing for an answer to Why? Finally, as he prayed, the answer came. All the Lord said was, *Trust me, Darrell. I have it all under control!*

I tried to imagine myself in Darrell's shoes, and I asked him, "Was that enough? To know that God was in control even though your circumstances never changed?"

Darrell responded by saying that he decided he had to take his eyes off his circumstances and focus them on the Lord. Time passed, and nothing changed. Darrell still had to live with nothing. He had to go to school wearing the same shirt, day in and day out all year long, and to sleep in the same cold, damp place night after night.

Although Darrell was laughed at and ridiculed, his perspective on life changed, and he experienced overwhelming peace and contentment. He survived the lonely days and nights with a song in his heart because he knew without doubt that Jesus loved and cared for him.

Darrell finished high school and went on to earn a theology degree from Criswell Bible College. When he was twenty-two, he met and married his wife. Today they have two children, and Darrell's vision of building his own church has become a reality.

Talking with Darrell Gilyard made me thirst after God's voice because I want to hear God as Darrell heard Him—with everything under control, even the things I can't explain. If ever there was a man who found out that life is tough but God is faithful, it is Darrell Gilyard. Nothing at all in his life made sense. There was no good news that he could see with his eyes, but he learned to live by faith, not by sight. He learned to live by what he knew was true because God had spoken it to his heart.

MANY QUESTIONS, FEW ANSWERS

Darrell Gilyard's story is dramatic, but what was true for him is true for you and me. No matter what kind of problem may land on our backs, all we finally have is Jesus, and He is worth it because He loves us.

Yes, we still have questions. Should we hesitate to ask them because we're supposed to have all the answers? Satan loves it when we are silent, afraid to ask the questions that can lead us to understanding. In his book *True Believers Don't Ask Why*, John Fischer wrote: "Jesus never hands truth to anyone. We must reach out and grasp it."[1]

I sometimes wonder why we aren't willing to ask more questions in our search to find the truth. Perhaps, as John Fischer suggested, we don't like questions because they "leave us vulnerable, weak, needy. They open up gaping holes in our personality, our theology, or our lifestyle. Questions force an honesty that we are unwilling to confront—an honesty that requires us to live with our lives unresolved."[2]

But living our lives with certain things unresolved is what faith is all about. I believe that many things happen that we simply can't explain. When we look back after many years, we still have little understanding of what went on. But we have the knowledge and assurance that Jesus was there with us through every moment, walking by our side, guiding our footsteps. We never needed to fear the questions, because Jesus was answer enough.

Some of the greatest words Paul ever wrote start with questions: Can anything separate us from the love Christ has for us? Can troubles or problems or sufferings? If we have no food or clothes, if we are in danger, or even if death comes, can any of these things separate us from Christ's love?

Paul's answer is that nothing—*absolutely nothing*—in this entire world can separate us from the love of God that is in Christ Jesus our Lord. "For I am persuaded," Paul said, "that neither death nor life, nor angels nor principalities, nor things present nor things to come, nor height nor depth, nor any other created thing, shall be able to separate us from the love of God" (Rom. 8:38–39 NKJV).

Here is where we must start. Even in the darkest night, the most blinding pain, the most maddening frustration—when nothing makes sense anymore—we keep going because He alone is worth it all.

For years I drank deeply of the false belief that if I just had enough faith everything would go my way. I thought I had God in a box: I do this for God and He does that for me. But it's not true, and so many lives are caught and wrecked in the wake of this teaching.

"What did I do wrong?" we cry. Heaven cries back, "Everything, but I love you anyway. Always have, always will."

Hannah Whitall Smith expressed God's love so well:

Put together all the tenderest love you know,
The deepest you have ever felt,
And the strongest that has ever been poured out
    upon you,
And heap upon it all the love of all the loving human
    hearts in the world,
And then multiply it by infinity,
And you will begin, perhaps,
To have some faint glimpse of the love God has for you.[3]

What an overwhelming statement! Does that seem real to you? Or do you read it as something that sounds great but when you look at your life it's as useful as a well-worn teabag? I am beginning to get it. Just beginning.

Holding on is hard—it can seem impossible—but it is worth it because Jesus is worth it. No matter what happens, Jesus is enough.

3

CLOUDED IMAGES

When low self-esteem and doubt paralyze us, we can give up and accept this clouded image, or we can remember who we are in Christ.

*I*n May 1986 I looked out the airplane window as the sun sparkled on the brilliant snow. "Ladies and gentlemen, we are about to land at Denver's Stapleton Airport. Please fasten your seat belts."

I had a concert that evening in a school auditorium. We'd had a pleasant flight, and I rested for a couple of hours in our hotel room before the evening began. A friend was promoting the concert, and so I felt at home.

A young local girl, Sarah, sang before it was my turn to sing. She was good, and the crowd liked her. I could see her genuine love for Christ sparkle in her eyes, and she had a beautiful voice. When she finished, my friend walked up to the microphone: "We'll take a short break for about ten minutes, and when we come back, Sheila Walsh will be with us."

Some in the audience clapped, while others rushed to the

24

rest rooms before the lines got too long. I shared a dressing room with the young singer, and she came bursting in.

"Wow, that was fun! Do you think I did okay?" she asked.

"I thought you were great, Sarah," I said. "The Lord really used you."

A couple of beaming faces appeared at the doorway. "Sheila," said Sarah, "this is my mom and dad."

We shook hands, and I could tell how proud they were of their "little girl." I stood by, enjoying the whole scene, but then I got my cue and told them I had to go. I almost got to the door when Sarah's father said, "Boy, your dad must be *so* proud of you."

I'm not sure why he said that. Perhaps he wanted to include me in the joy he felt about his own daughter. I know he meant what he said as a compliment, but I felt as if I had been kicked in the stomach. Without replying, I turned and pulled the door shut behind me. I didn't want them to see my face. I didn't want them to ask questions.

Your dad must be so proud of you . . . The words brought everything back. Why, after all these years, could it still hurt so badly? Would I ever be completely free? I sat in a rest room cubicle with my head in my hands. What would it have been like if my dad had lived? Would my life have been different? Would I have been a different person? How I wanted him to be standing there that night to be proud of me, but he had been gone for a long time.

I stepped out on the stage, and I knew the only way I could get myself together was to do what I always do—be very honest with the crowd and share my heart.

"You know," I told them, "a strange thing happened to

me just a few minutes ago . . ." I went on to talk about the incident in the dressing room. I talked about the things that hurt us, the things that wound us, and the things we don't understand.

I shared just a bit from my childhood—how my father had been such a wonderful Christian man who was so much fun to be with. Then one night he went to bed as warm and loving as ever, but woke up a changed man. A brain thrombosis had left him weak and confused, and for the next eleven months our family had to watch as he deteriorated before our eyes.

I didn't say much more and quickly went on with the concert, but that scene in the dressing room stayed with me. I realized that even though I had dealt with certain things in my life, the memories were still there, waiting to remind me of the pain that had invaded my childhood and changed my life forever.

THE LAST GOOD CHRISTMAS

I was born in Cumnock, a small mining town near the western coast of Scotland. Mum was a straight arrow who had loved God most of her life, never veering to the right or left. Dad's path had been a rockier one. He had served with the British Navy and, like many young sailors, he'd "lived" a little. But when he finally gave his heart to God, he gave it all.

My dad had a very practical faith. If he saw someone with real need, he did something about it. He didn't just pray, he was prepared to be the answer to his own prayers. He was spontaneous and a lot of fun. I thought he was wonderful.

My sister, Frances, who is two years older than I, was a contented and placid child, unlike me. I was a tomboy, and when I reached my third birthday, I wanted a dog very badly. I wanted my own living, barking Lassie who would rescue me from any perilous situation, and there were many of those in my life!

One evening, when Frances and I were tucked in bed wearing our pajamas, our father came into our room.

"Sheila," he said, "I want you to close your eyes and hold out your hands." I obeyed, and as I stuck out my hands, something furry ran up my sleeve. I screamed and jumped out of bed, running frantically about, trying to free myself from what felt like a rat.

"Be careful, be careful!" Mum cried. "It's a little puppy!"

I sat with eyes like saucers as Mum extracted the little dog from my pajama sleeve. It was a baby dachshund, and we decided to call her Heidi. It was just before Christmas, and my life seemed so complete. Mum had just given birth to a beautiful little boy they named Stephen. What more could we ask for!

Well, there was one more thing—a dollhouse, which I'd always wanted. It must have cost Dad quite a bit. As a traveling salesman from our farming community, he never made a lot of money, but he always provided for us.

That Christmas, however, he somehow managed to come up with the money for the dollhouse, and I thought it was the most wonderful Christmas I had ever had.

It would be the last Christmas I had with my father at home. Just a few weeks later, the father I knew was gone forever, stolen by a thrombosis in his brain that struck in the night. His power of speech was gone, and he was paralyzed down one side.

LIFE CHANGED COMPLETELY FOR ALL OF US

I don't remember very much about the next year or so. Everything was changed, nothing was sure, and life was sometimes confusing. Trapped in his stroke-crippled body, my father never spoke a word. Instead he communicated with unintelligible noises. He was able to move about with a cane, and most of the time he seemed very weak. Like most small children, I adapted quickly to my father's condition and would sit on his knee to read to him from my storybooks and tell him what I had been doing that day. I believed my dad still loved me and still understood me.

But as the months went by, my father went from being a warm and gentle hiding place for me to acting at times cold and unpredictable. He began to have what I would call "brain storms," which put him into a rage and gave him the strength of three men. Later, when he came out of them, he would realize what he had done and sit holding his head in his hands, crying like a child.

For some reason, he directed most of his anger toward me, never toward Frances or Stephen. Sometimes he would look at me as if he hated me. I didn't know why. I was only four years old. I guessed that there had to be something horribly wrong with me; otherwise, why would my dad look at me like that?

One day, not long before I was to turn four, I sat by the fire playing with Heidi, the little puppy he had given me the

Christmas before. I looked up and saw my dad coming toward me with a strange look in his eyes.

He raised his cane, and at that moment I knew that he was going to hit me. In sheer panic, I pulled the cane away from him, and he lost his balance and fell. He lay there moaning, and I was sure it was all my fault. Mum rushed in to help him, and I ran to my room and hid, trembling and afraid to come out.

Eventually it became necessary for my dad to be admitted to a psychiatric hospital, for his well-being and for ours.

My father hung on for a few more months, and then he went "home," at peace at last with the Lord. But in my little heart, there was no peace. I would wake up in the night, crying, "O God, why am I so miserable? I hate myself." Somewhere in my heart a door slammed shut, and I buried a piece of my life for many years.

MUM MANAGED WITH A MEAGER INCOME

Left with three children under the age of seven, my mum's prayer was, "God, I pray You will spare me to see Frances, Sheila, and Stephen grow up to love and trust You. That's all I ask."

With no income, Mum decided that we should move back to Ayr, where she was raised, into a government-owned "Council House"—one of the homes people on a low income could rent at a reasonable rate. The government also gave Mum what was called a "widow's pension," about sixteen pounds (twenty-eight dollars) a week, which she went down to collect every Tuesday morning. I remember distinctly that it was a Tuesday because sometimes we didn't have any toilet tissue left by Monday night!

There was never enough to pay the bills, but Mum managed somehow. She was careful with every penny, and members of the church we attended would help from time to time. Because her health wasn't the best after Dad died, Mum never went back to work. She made do with her meager pension, kept our home nice for all of us, and was always there when we came home from school.

My father's stroke, frightening rages, and eventual death seemed to affect me more than it did anyone else in the family. I would sit in church on Sunday and listen to the pastor say, "For those of you who have lost a husband or a dad or a mum, you can rejoice that one day you'll see them again."

But I didn't want to see my dad again. I was afraid of him.

For years after my father died, I kept having the same nightmare: I saw him coming to get me because I had pushed his cane away and made him fall that day. I often woke up in the middle of the night, crying into my pillow, and I also walked in my sleep until I was sixteen. I changed from a happy, outgoing, friendly little girl to a loner who was withdrawn and introspective. I never let Mum out of my sight and was with her every possible minute.

To my family it seemed as if I would never be "normal"—that I would never want to venture outside of my home alone, and I would always be afraid.

But Mum did not believe that. She would get down on her knees and pray, "God, You're bigger than this thing. And I ask that You would glorify Yourself through my daughter."

Mum was an incredible inspiration to us all. She believed God would provide what we needed, and she prayed for those needs with simple faith. She never got bitter or angry with God over her lot. She was like a rock for our family, and her faith kept us strong. She knew that God is faithful.

BEYOND THE HERE AND NOW

It's often tough to see beyond the present circumstance. When you've lost a job and don't know if you will be able to find another one before your immediate funds run out. Or when your boyfriend or spouse says, "I don't love you anymore. Let's call it quits." That's when we feel that God is not faithful. Some of us would look at Job's incredible disaster, pain, and suffering and say that God is not faithful. But God did set boundaries on what Satan could do to Job.

First He told Satan, "You can do anything you like with his wealth, but don't harm him physically." And even though Job lost all his wealth and his sons and daughters, he withstood Satan's first test. Instead of cursing God, he responded to his tragedy by saying, "I came naked from my mother's womb, and I shall have nothing when I die. The Lord gave me everything I had, and they were His to take away."

But Satan does not want to lose any battle for our souls. The next time he approached the throne of God, he argued for one more test. "A man will give anything to save his life," he said. "Touch his body with sickness and he will curse you to your face."

God allowed Satan this final challenge, but again He set a boundary. "Do with him as you please, only spare his life."

God did set boundaries on Job's testing. And I believe

that He also sets boundaries on ours. Scripture says, "God is faithful, who will not allow you to be tempted beyond what you are able, but with the temptation will also make the way of escape, that you may be able to bear it" (1 Cor. 10:13 NKJV).

Still you might see God as a cruel taskmaster for allowing Satan to inflict Job with both these incredible disasters. Yet God knew the outcome. Unfortunately Job didn't. Neither do we.

Still we often wish we *did* know the outcome of our lives. Then we could see the rainbow at the end of the storm. Certainly I thought this later in my life when I was overwhelmed by my unbelievable schedule cohosting *700 Club* during the week and traveling throughout the country doing concerts on the weekend.

Yet I realize the arrogance of this wish. We are asking to be like God. And we would probably be tempted to try to change the course of our lives by making different decisions along the way. "I don't think I'll marry this guy, because it will lead me to that." Or "I won't take this job, because they are going to lay me off anyway when the recession hits."

I wonder if this desire to know the future is what got Eve into trouble in the first place. She wanted to be like God. She wanted to be wise. Might she also have wanted to know the future? Maybe.

I now realize it's a blessing that we don't know what lies ahead. If I had seen the years between then and now—the days when I was hospitalized for severe clinical depression, the year afterward as I tried to hold on to my healing and understand how I might again serve the Lord (and who I was when I no longer cohosted the *700 Club*)—I might have been thrown into a depression that would have destroyed me. Even if I could have seen the promise of my life at the end of the tunnel, would I have been strong enough to have lived through those four years? I don't know.

And if I had been strong enough, God still wouldn't have had the opportunity to see how his servant Sheila would react to this test in her life. Would I keep on keeping on because I knew God is faithful?

At first Job held on to his faith in a faithful God, even though he couldn't see the rainbow after the storm. When his exasperated wife threw up her hands in desperation and said, "Curse God and die," Job replied, "What? Shall we receive only pleasant things from the hand of God and never anything unpleasant?"(Job 2:10 TLB).

The Scripture verse then asserts: "So in all this Job said nothing wrong." Job knew God is faithful.

And so did my mum. Because she knew God is faithful, He answered her prayer to "glorify Yourself through my daughter."

When I was eleven, an evangelist came to our town. I remember hearing him explain that God had no grandchildren—only sons and daughters. Many people went forward, but I just couldn't move. That night, however, I told my mum I wanted to become a Christian. We knelt together in my bedroom, and Mum prayed with me as I became a child of God.

I COULDN'T CALL GOD "FATHER"

Strangely enough, however, I could not pray to God as my Father. I was still trying to bury my dad's tragedy deep inside. I blotted out that horrible night when they took my dad away, and I substituted my own fantasy: My father and I were walking along the beach and suddenly he was "taken home." There was no pain or screaming or fear—nothing like that to deal with. My dad had just gone home. I knew where he'd gone, and it was fine with me.

Throughout my teenage years it seemed we had an unwritten rule in our family not to talk too much about my dad because I couldn't handle it. At times I would fall into deep depression as I tried to cope alone with my bottled-up feelings. Sometimes I would sit staring straight ahead as my mum begged me to talk to her and not shut her out. Inside, I felt like screaming, but I just couldn't express my feelings. I felt as if I had fallen into a pit too deep to crawl out of, and no one could reach me.

While I coped with my inner turmoil, life went on, and much of it was good. As I entered my teens, my singing voice showed promise, and I started taking private lessons from a wonderful man named Mr. Tweddle. He was a perfectionist. After my first lesson he said, "Sheila, you sound like a cross between a sheep and a machine gun."

Mr. Tweddle assigned strange exercises, like singing an incredible assortment of different phrases over and over. For a while I wasn't sure Mr. Tweddle knew what he was doing. But when he entered me in a music festival competition in which I won first place in two categories, I changed my mind in a hurry! Singing became a tremendous outlet for me. I went from being a fearful little girl who wouldn't leave my mum's side to performing in front of people—and really enjoying it!

Mr. Tweddle wanted me to train for opera, but I headed

in a different direction when a gospel group called Unity invited me to join them. For two years, fifteen of us traveled all over Scotland on weekends and school holidays, singing and giving our testimonies.

One evening it was my turn to speak. I prayed for an hour before the concert, asking for the right words to say. Petrified, I talked for about fifteen minutes and, incredibly, fourteen young people became Christians that night. I was so ecstatic I couldn't sleep. That experience helped me to decide that with God it would be all or nothing. I had to tell Mr. Tweddle I could not be an opera singer, that I planned to be a missionary.

At the age of sixteen, I stood on the beach of our small fishing town and said, "Lord, I'm all Yours. But I've nothing to give You. I'm an emotional wreck. I'm afraid of boys. I'm afraid of everything. I know I'm ugly. I hate myself, Lord. But if You can do anything with me, I'm Yours."

During the next couple of years my friends and I would go downtown at night and talk to people on the streets. Some of them were kids and some were adults who had become alcoholics, but they all had one thing in common: They had no hope. They were the kind of people my dad would help whenever he had the chance. In a way, we carried on where my dad left off.

———

Turning Point: When low self-esteem and doubt paralyze us, we can give up and accept this clouded image, or we can remember who we are in Christ.

———

I was beginning to know who I was in Christ, just as
Sandra Cerda finally did.

INSIDE OUT

As a child Sandra Cerda felt like nobody. Her mother abandoned her when Sandra was four years old. Her grandpar-
ents took her in, but her grandfather began sexually abusing
her and her life became a nightmare. Every night she lay in
bed, shivering, afraid, and ashamed. She longed to be loved
but felt unlovable and unclean.

At fifteen years old, with visions of that elusive white
picket fence and peaceful home, Sandra married. But her
dream quickly dissipated. Her husband turned out to be a
violent man who constantly beat her. When she was three
months pregnant, he beat her with a plank of wood and she
finally left him. Once again Sandra was nobody. No one she
knew had compassion or pity on her.

Sandra found work as a topless dancer in a bar. She
longed for love and acceptance and looked for it in the eyes
of the men in the bar. Not finding the love she sought,
Sandra decided to find a more respected profession.

Sandra began modeling for newspaper ads and commer-
cials, a career in which she excelled. She eventually gained a
coveted spot in a national swimsuit magazine, and people frequently complimented her on her beauty. Yet, inside, she felt
ugly and alone. Sandra began using crack cocaine to stop the
pain, but the crack couldn't change her identity—she was still
a lost little girl. Even though she had beautiful clothes and
carefully applied makeup, Sandra still felt she was nobody.

A severe case of skin cancer changed Sandra's life. Sandra has shown me pictures of the infected skin that covered her body and left her unable to look at herself in the mirror. She received radiation treatment, but the cancer only grew worse. Sandra's doctors finally gave up on her. But before she gave up on herself, Sandra remembered a female relative who always seemed to have peace in her life. She was never as attractive as Sandra had been, but grace seemed to rest on her. So Sandra went to visit with her.

Sandra's relative not only revealed the source of peace in her life—God—but she told Sandra this same God longed to treat Sandra with kindness and compassion. Sandra wept as she heard about the love of Christ. She asked Him to forgive her for four abortions and a godless lifestyle.

All of her life Sandra had tried to fit in, to belong. She had looked unsuccessfully for acceptance in her family and through her work. The approval she received because of her beauty gave her a glimmer of hope. But that hope didn't keep her from feeling alone. And the cancer robbed her of even that little hope.

Now, in her least attractive state, she who felt like nobody became somebody. When Sandra met the Lord, she discovered that He had chosen her and longed to show her His kindness. She had done nothing to attract His attention. She could do nothing to lose it. Sandra had been searching for a little pity, but instead she found an identity, a sense of belonging, and a purpose for her life. She discovered that, as a believer, she was part of "a chosen generation, a royal priesthood, a holy nation, [God's] own special people," whose purpose was to proclaim God's praise. This, according to Peter in his first epistle, is the security all believers have.

Beauty is fragile and temporary. A life built on beauty alone will disappear as quickly as a home built of ice when the summer is coming. A life built on the love of God, however, will flourish and will weather loneliness and trials because the love of God lasts forever.

God has completely healed Sandra. Her face is lovely again, but the beauty she exudes comes from the peace of knowing she has been found.

4

No Hidden Places

When guilt occupies the secret places in our lives, we can let it cripple us, or we can allow God to set us free.

J didn't understand it at the time, but my mind and emotions were really running on two different tracks way back in 1972, when I was a teenager. Part of me was a fervent teen who wanted to serve God, and the other part was a frightened little girl who felt guilty because she had pulled her father's cane out from under him, made him fall, and then watched as he screamed out in rage. Had I caused my father's death? Had I made him hate me? I had never been sure, and the best way I could cope with growing up was to bottle it up inside.

When I was nineteen, I enrolled at London Bible College to study to be a missionary. I had decided that because a woman couldn't be a minister, the next best thing would be missionary work, going off into the bush somewhere and reaching the unreached with the gospel. Actually, I didn't want to be a missionary that badly. I didn't want to go far from home, but I did want God to love me always. I really loved the Lord, but at the same time I felt I had to earn His love. I never wanted Him to turn away from me.

Some of my friends would fall away at times, but I was determined that this would never happen to me. I'd tell God, "I'll never do this, Lord. I'll always hang in there. You'll always have me; I'll always love You."

As I look back on my college years, I can see that part of my motivation was really wanting to serve God, but also driving me was the fact that I wanted to push myself harder than anybody else to prove to God that I was worthy of His love. My hidden places controlled my life, but I didn't realize it. I knew God, but I still needed a freeing touch from Him. In many ways, I was like the searching people Jesus met as He walked the dusty roads of Palestine, individuals whose hidden places kept them trapped in lives they longed to change.

We all know the story of the Samaritan woman. Sometimes we don't realize how typical she is of each of us. Surely she longed for a different life, with no hidden places, no secrets, no lying awake at night wondering where it all had gone wrong. Guilt crippled her, but she was able to free herself from its grasp.

Jesus unlocked her secret with just one statement: "Go and get your husband and come back and we can talk."

The Samaritan woman hung her head for a second as all the ugliness paraded before her eyes, and then she looked at Jesus. The time for hiding was over.

"Sir, I don't have a husband."

As Jesus looked into the very soul of this lonely, beaten

woman, He saw all the sin and guilt, and He loved her. "I know," He said. "You've had five husbands, and you're not married to the man you're living with now."

There it was, out in the sunlight, revealed by Jesus' truthful, but compassionate, words. As she looked at Jesus, the woman realized that she didn't have to run anymore. He knew it all, and yet He loved her. Surely, this Man was a prophet. He had found her hidden places, her addiction to empty, meaningless relationships. All her life she had looked for someone to fill the void.

I am sure that many of us identify with that woman's story. There are few people who have no hidden places. Some reach for a bottle of Scotch when the pain gets too much. Others are trapped in an endless cycle of food binges to dull the self-hatred and loneliness. And many lash out or hide or find themselves driven because of things they suffered as a child.

Yet we all have a choice, just as the Samaritan woman had a choice. When guilt occupies the secret places in our lives, we can let it cripple us or we can allow the painful, healing light of God's love to set us free. The Samaritan woman believed she knew God and how to worship Him, but Jesus cut through her theology to get to the real point. Those who worship God must worship Him in spirit and in truth (John 4:24).

Turning Point: When guilt occupies the secret places in our lives, we can let it cripple us, or we can allow God to set us free.

It was then that the woman knew that she was speaking with the Messiah. She chose to "come clean," to open all the doors of her secret past and step completely into the sunlight. Satan revels in planting his seeds in the shadowy places of our lives. His bitter fruit only grows in dark, musty places, and when the sunlight falls upon his evil crop, it withers and dies.

We never hear again of that woman. Perhaps she stood with the crowds on Golgotha hill that terrible day and watched. As the sky grew dark, she must have thought back to how it used to be, before she had met Him. She had not been the same since the light of His love had pierced her darkness. No longer could the enemy torment her with her worthlessness. She had looked in the face of God, and He was smiling.

GOD FINALLY DID A "NEW THING" FOR ME

I had known the story of the Samaritan woman since childhood, but as I grew up I didn't realize how much we had in common. As my college years flew by, I was so busy with studies, prayer meetings, and going out with evangelistic teams that I suppose I became quite sure that I had dealt with my father's death. But the guilt and fear still lay buried deep inside. Whether praying alone or with friends, I continued the habit I had started as a young girl, seldom addressing God as Father. The only exception was when I would quote the Lord's Prayer. Then I would use the phrase "Our Father, who art in heaven," but otherwise I always addressed my prayers to "Jesus" or "the Lord."

I never noticed this, and if someone had brought it to my attention I probably would have said I had no problem with God being our heavenly Father. I just felt very close to Jesus because He is our Savior and Friend.

Something else I didn't notice was how the burden I carried inside affected my relationships with the opposite sex. London Bible College was a great spot to be a girl, because there were two men to every woman and they were all Christians. I dated a few times during my first years of school, but none of those relationships was serious. My senior year, however, was different. Dave was all I would ever want—or so I thought.

We were assigned to the same evangelistic team. He preached and I sang. I guess I thought we would make a perfect couple, serving the Lord somewhere after we got married. But our relationship didn't last. As much as I loved Dave, something made me afraid to get totally involved with anyone. I believed that if you gave yourself totally to someone, you gave that person the power to hurt and even break you. What I didn't understand completely was that this philosophy had come out of the terrible hurt I had experienced with my father.

I might have gone on like this for many more years, perhaps for life, had it not been for one special day during my senior year. Each term we had a Quiet Day with no lectures or regular class activities. We went to chapel in the morning and evening, and we were free to spend the rest of the time alone with the Lord. During morning chapel, the speaker's text had been Isaiah 43:18–21. For some reason, verses 18 and 19 burned into my memory:

The Lord says, "Forget what happened before, and do not think about the past. Look at the new thing I am going to do. It is already happening. Don't you see it?" (NCV).

After chapel I walked alone in some woods near our dorm with my Bible and my daily study notes. I turned to the passage assigned for the day. Throughout the day I pondered why Isaiah 43:18–19 had hit me so hard. What was I supposed to forget, and what new thing was God doing that I didn't see yet?

I was still thinking about those verses after going back to my room, when one of my friends came by to give me a gift. She had copied down Isaiah 43:18 in her exquisite copperplate script. As I admired her lovely work, I knew that God must be trying to tell me something. To that point, however, I wasn't getting the message. My past was a closed book. It had nothing to do with any new thing that God might be planning for me.

At 10:00 that night I was in the Student Common Room watching the late news when for no apparent reason tears welled up in my eyes. I rushed back to my room, fell on my bed, and wept for over an hour. Some kind of groaning was coming from deep inside me, but I couldn't identify the cause of my grief.

Around midnight I went down the hall to talk to Jenny, who served as a student leader of our dorm. "I don't know what's happening," I told her. "There's something happening to me, and I don't know what to do. I feel as though I can hardly bear it." Jenny didn't know me very well, but she suggested that we get down on our knees and pray together. After we prayed for some time, she said, "You know, I think God is trying to tell you something about your father."

I let out a groan that was almost a roar of pain. The house where we had lived before my father's stroke and death flashed into my mind. Again I saw his confused and angry face as he came at me with that cane. I realized that something had been locked away inside. I had shut a door, and there was no way that I was going to let anyone in to this part of my life—not even God.

As I prayed with Jenny, I was able to face the hurt that I had refused to admit was even there. For the first time I realized that ever since becoming a Christian as a young girl I had rarely called God *Father*. Now I understood why. The pain caused by my own father's death had been too much to bear, and I didn't want to link God with that.

I went back to my room and spent most of the rest of the night with a concordance and my Bible, looking up verses referring to God as Father and weeping for joy over each one.

Mum and I Needed to Talk

The next day I knew what I had to do. I went to see Mr. Kirby, our principal. I knew he would understand. Of all the people I met at London Bible College—and I thank God for every one of them—I am most thankful for Gilbert Kirby, and he is my good friend to this day. Well-read and wise, he always retains a childlike wonder at the mystery of the gospel.

I guess I looked pretty awful because I had been up all night crying, but Mr. Kirby listened carefully as I told him what had happened. Finally I said, "You know, I think I should go home. After all these years, my mum and I have never been able to really talk about my dad. I've never even had a photo of my dad. I never wanted one. But now Mum and I need to talk."

"I think it's a great idea," he said without hesitation. "I think you should do that immediately. Here, let me find out when the next train leaves."

Mr. Kirby asked his secretary to call and get the train schedule. I packed a few things quickly and walked down to the station, which was only three minutes away. The four-hundred-fifty-mile trip from London to Ayr took over six hours. I spent the time reading the Bible, praying, and trying to think about what I would say to Mum—what I would ask her after all these years.

When she opened the door, her face was a mixture of surprised joy and wondering if something was seriously wrong. I said, "Hi, Mum . . . I had to come home because . . ." Then I burst into tears. For several minutes I couldn't gather the words to tell her what had happened. All I could say was, "It's all right . . . I'm okay. I'm okay."

She made me a cup of tea and, although she was anxious and puzzled, waited for me to gather myself together enough to tell her what had happened. I told her the whole story, especially the part about seeing our home flash before my eyes when Jenny said, "I think God is trying to tell you something about your father."

I described to Mum the picture of our home that had come into my mind, and she said, "Yes, that's what it was like . . . That's where we lived."

And then we talked for a long time about things I had never wanted to know before, about how things had been while my father was in the psychiatric hospital in those months before he died. Mum told me everything, describing her feelings during my father's illness, the sense of emptiness when he died. She told me about the funeral and where my dad was buried. She described at length how hard it had been to commit Dad to a psychiatric hospital.

"I wonder at times if I held on to him too long," she admitted, "but it was so hard to let him go because he was my husband, and I loved him so much."

All that day and into the evening we talked, looked through photograph albums, and cried together. I stayed with Mum until Monday morning before taking the train back to school. My weekend with her had been a wonderful time of healing. The fear and guilt that had festered inside me ever since I was four years old was beginning to cleanse away. I realized that what had happened to my dad was not his fault—and it certainly was not mine. I finally understood that pulling away his cane and making him fall was not an unforgivable sin, but only the act of a frightened little girl who couldn't understand what had happened to her dad.

The English poet John Donne wrote: "Look, Lord, and find both Adams met in me. As the first Adam's sweat surrounds my face, may the last Adam's blood my soul embrace." After that weekend, I could embrace the last Adam's blood with new and much deeper gratitude. Now I understood the message God had for me in Isaiah: "Do not think about the past. Look at the new thing I am going to do."

I could walk away from the past and concentrate on what God was going to do with my future, because I had allowed His love to set me free.

SO MANY HIDE BEHIND
THEIR WOUNDS

Over the years I've learned that my story is not unique. Many people have secret places where they hide and lick their wounds. They choose to live a life of denial and doubt rather than be honest with themselves. Sometimes they are unaware of what they're hiding, or why.

For so many of us, it takes years to come face-to-face with the fears that lurk in our past. We bury them so deeply because we are convinced that if they were released they would overwhelm us. We don't allow ourselves to think about them even for a moment, but their long shadows cast a dark cloud over our minds nonetheless.

The Greek word for *salvation* means "to save, to heal, to make complete." That is what happens at the cross. The Father is committed to shining His light into the darkest corners where fear and sorrow lurk and bringing peace.

Unfortunately, you can know the joy of salvation but not always let God shine His light everywhere He would like. And where you leave hidden areas, the enemy has a home, a foothold to claw at your heart.

One of my favorite passages of Scripture comes from 2 Corinthians, where Paul spoke from personal experience: "We have troubles all around us, but we are not defeated. We do not know what to do, but we do not give up the hope of living. We are persecuted, but God does not leave us. We are hurt sometimes, but we are not destroyed" (4:8–9 NCV). Paul's words remind me of a wonderful song by Phil McHugh, the chorus of which says:

In heaven's eyes, there are no losers,
In heaven's eyes, no hopeless cause
Just people like you with feelings like me
Amazed by the grace that we have found in heaven's eyes.[1]

I enjoyed and appreciated every person I interviewed on *Heart to Heart*, but every now and then, there were people who were special. There was something about them that makes you want to wrap them up and take them home.

THE MORNING AFTER

Al Kasha is that kind of person—so warm and real. I admire him as a songwriter too. He won an Academy Award for best song written for a movie for "The Morning After," which he wrote with Joel Hirschhorn. It became the theme for the film *The Poseidon Adventure*.

I can still remember seeing *The Poseidon Adventure* with my mum in a little Scottish theater that always showed a double feature. Somehow I got the times confused, and my mum and I had to suffer through two and a half hours of the worst John Wayne movie ever made before *The Poseidon Adventure* came on at 9:25 P.M. But we loved the film, and I rode home on the bus with Mum that night, humming, "There's got to be a morning after . . ."

It turns out that Al Kasha wrote that song out of a very personal experience. He was brought up in a poor family, living above a barbershop in Brooklyn with his brother and an incredibly cruel father. His dad was an alcoholic, who on the nights when he got very, very drunk would come home and beat Al and his brother.

He once left Al locked up in a closet and didn't remember to let him out until three days later. Al's childhood was a nightmare. In high school he got a role in the school production of *Oklahoma* and was very excited to be singing and just to be part of the whole thing. His father burst into the school theater, drunk, and caused a terrible scene. Later on, Al's father beat him badly for daring to be ashamed of how his father had embarrassed him. One day, Al had had enough. When his father tried to abuse him, Al struck back and knocked his father down and left home, never to go back.

Al's mother didn't abuse him physically, but her treatment was perhaps even more damaging. She found it hard to express her feelings. She could never tell Al, "You're doing a good job; I'm proud of you." Instead, she pushed and pushed Al to achieve and do better and better. He isn't sure, but perhaps she felt that if she ever told him, "You know, you've really done it. I'm proud of you," she would no longer control him.

As I talked with Al on *Heart to Heart* in 1990, I told him I had watched the Academy Awards when "The Morning After" had been nominated. I was nervous, as I always am every year when I watch the awards ceremony. My palms sweat, and I'm not even nominated for anything! Every time somebody wins, I feel as if that person is my brother or my sister, and I practically burst for joy even though we have never met.

When "The Morning After" won and Al's name was announced, I imagined how thrilled he was when he went forward to get his Oscar. Little did I know that he was already battling the anxieties suffered by every victim of agoraphobia, fear of open places. Agoraphobics become so afraid that they want to lock themselves away in a corner and hide from the world because they just hurt too much.

Al marched up to the stage that night with Joel Hirschhorn, his cowriter. Al smiled and gave his acceptance speech, but his heart was pounding, and he was terrified that he might break down right there in front of the sophisticated Hollywood crowd.

He got through it, however, and afterward he wondered what his brother, Larry, thought. A Broadway producer, Larry had already won a Tony for *Applause*, a show starring Lauren Bacall. Al knew that Larry was his mother's favorite, although she denied it.

The next day the phone rang, and Al heard his mother's voice gushing with excitement, "L'Alfred, I'm so proud of you!"

"*Alfred*, Mom." Al couldn't help correcting her. Since Larry was always on her mind, she had a tendency to combine their names.

"An Oscar! And someday I'll bet you win a second Oscar!"

The blood drained from Al's face, and he gasped for breath. A second Oscar! The gold plating on the first was still fresh.

His mother's next statement lodged like a bullet in his brain and stayed there for the next ten years. "And someday, L'Alfred darling, you'll really make it, when you win a Tony, like your brother did."[2]

Al went on to plunge into his work even further, winning another Oscar for "We May Never Love Like This Again," the theme for the film *Towering Inferno*. But it was never enough, and he fell deeper and deeper into depression. When his father died of cancer, the symptoms of his agoraphobia became overwhelming. He began to have heart palpitations, and he hyperventilated when he was out in a restaurant or anywhere away from home. Soon he refused to go out to work, to appointments, anywhere.

Eventually, his wife, Ceil, could stand it no longer, and she asked him to leave. After being separated for about a month, they met to talk about reconciliation. After their meeting, Al went home, his palpitations worse than ever. He had been trying to get treatment for his agoraphobia, but in a fit of self-reproach for being weak, he had stopped going to group therapy meetings.

Al arrived home and was in such total despair that his body was trembling as tears rolled down his cheeks. Suddenly he said, "God, if You're listening, help me." He didn't feel he deserved God's love, but he ached for it. He flipped on the television set, and a fuzzy picture of the Reverend Robert Schuller flashed on the screen. Then he heard the words, "Perfect love casts out all fear."

At first Al dismissed the words as too simplistic, but then his mind reversed them, and he found himself thinking, "Fear casts out all love." He realized that that was what had happened to him. Fear *had* cast out all love. He had been afraid to fail—his wife, his child, his partner, his parents, the artists he worked with, and his friends. He'd found it easier to imprison himself behind his phobias, hiding from the world.

Al continued to watch the Schuller broadcast. He heard the words, "If you put your trust in Him, you'll find more peace than you've ever known." It dawned on him that his only hope was to get the focus off himself and put it somewhere else. He realized he didn't have to be perfect and take all the responsibility. He only had to be real and honest, and all God was asking from him was to do his best.

There in his room in front of the television set, Al uttered one word, *Jesus*. He kept repeating that same word, and as he did so, his fear diminished and peace started to fill his heart. He remembers, "I had a sense that a blinding light was filling the room. It seemed to me as if a window had opened. Whether the window of my soul or an actual window, I've never been quite sure. But there was an opening, a healing, a flowering inside that flooded my heart."[3]

With the television set still on, Al closed his eyes and fell asleep. The next morning he asked Jesus into his heart, and he was like a bird let out of a cage.

Al later reunited with his wife, and they both made public commitments to Christ at a nearby church. Slowly, he learned to conquer his fears by putting total trust in Christ. Today his anxiety attacks are gone.

Al wrote the words to "The Morning After" many years before he met Jesus, but they were to become words that fit his own life perfectly:

> There's got to be a morning after,
> If we can hold on through the night.
> We have a chance to find the sunshine;
> Let's keep on looking for the light.[4]

Al Kasha found the Light. He let Christ shine in his hidden places, and he's never been the same since.

5

LIVING SACRIFICES DON'T
CRAWL AWAY

===

*When the heat of problems and pain burns into our
very souls, we can crawl away and hide when it gets
too hot, or we can choose to be living sacrifices who
stay on the altar for His sake.*

*I*n the fall of 1991 I was sitting in my dressing
room at 9:00 one morning when Cheryl Gardener,
the producer of *Heart to Heart,* came in to talk
about that morning's program.

"Sheila, I want you to look at this," Cheryl said, showing me a photograph of a good-looking, tall Washington
state trooper. He looked as if he was in his late twenties,
early thirties.

"He looks like a nice man," I commented.

"Nice, he is. I just hope you won't be too shocked when
you meet him. He doesn't look like this anymore."

When I saw Michael, I was horrified. I couldn't recognize him from the picture.

Michael and I sat down to talk, and he took me back to the day of his accident. He had become a Christian just a few months before. He had started a Bible study and was excited about this new adventure in his life. The future looked bright, and Michael was on top of the world.

One day when Michael was on patrol, a drunk driver tore past him. He called for backup and began to chase this out-of-control car. The impaired driver made it halfway through a curve before he hit an oncoming vehicle and knocked it out of its lane and into Michael's car. Michael tried to avoid hitting the hurled vehicle, but he couldn't. His car burst into flames.

The firemen arrived at Michael's blazing vehicle and, assuming he was dead, began to put out the inferno. When the rescue team saw that Michael was alive, they cut him out of his car and rushed him to the hospital. Michael had second-, third-, and fourth-degree burns on fifty percent of his body. His bulletproof vest had protected his chest. But the doctors told his family that if he lived, they would have to amputate his left leg and both arms.

Michael lived. The amputations were performed. As Michael was slipping in and out of a drug-induced stupor, he prayed, "God, you have spared me for a reason. I trust You to show me that reason."

As a result of the accident, Michael's face is distorted, and one of his ears is completely gone. He has no hair, and the skin around his eyes is badly scarred and melted—it looks as if it is painful just to open his eyes. Who would blame Michael if he wanted to hide away in a darkened room? Who would wonder if he questioned the love and care of this heavenly Father he had just discovered?

OUR SENSE OF RIGHT IS BUILT IN

There is something built into every human being that says, "I have rights!" When we read in Romans 12:1 that all Christians are "living sacrifices," it sounds so noble. We hold on to that wonderful thought without ever wondering what the implications might be. When Paul used the words *living sacrifices,* he meant something much different from the old system.

In the Old Testament, a lamb was not consulted as to how it felt about being offered as a sacrifice. It was simply slaughtered and laid on the altar to be consumed by the fire. But in the New Testament—the New Covenant—we are living sacrifices. The trouble is, a living sacrifice can crawl off the altar when it gets too hot. God could have preprogrammed us as robots who serve Him without choice, but instead He has given us the ability to choose.

The more I walk with the Lord, the more I understand that every day of my life, for the rest of my walk on this earth, I can choose to stay on the altar or to crawl away. When the heat is turned up, I can crawl off and say, "Well, this is not what I signed up for. I thought that this would make me feel good. I thought that all my prayers would be answered, but it seems as if God has turned a deaf ear to my cry."

Suffering is seldom an item on our list of requests to the Lord. But when it crosses our path and we are able by His grace to keep on walking, our lives become messages of hope to the world and to the church. Besides Job, there are plenty of examples in Scripture of people who suffered physical pain or loss and spiritual persecution. David suffered politically and spiritually. He was chased by Saul's men, captured by the Philistines, and threatened by the followers of Baal. The apostle Peter, who lived in the New Testament era during a period of intense religious persecution, was eventually martyred upside down on a cross. In each case, we read of these men's commitment to God and their understanding that God's glory would be seen through their sufferings.

David lived on the run. He was captured and held prisoner by the Philistines. He was threatened by Saul and pursued by Saul's army. He suffered the torment of the followers of Baal. Yet, amidst his torment, he turned to God:

> Vows made to You are binding upon me, O God;
> I will render praises to You,
> For You have delivered my soul from death.
> Have You not kept my feet from falling,
> That I may walk before God
> In the light of the living? (Ps. 56:12–13 NKJV).

David's response to his suffering was similar to that of Michael, the state trooper. "God, You have spared me for a reason." David was thankful God had saved him, and he recognized God's purpose for him as he went on living: to "walk before God." David believed his purpose in this life was to be faithful to God and to honor Him. And his faithfulness would cause others to honor God.

Michael now travels across America to schools and colleges, telling his story. He lifts his head high and tells young people everywhere that although his body is burned, his faith in Christ is alive and well. Michael is overjoyed that Christ's glory is revealed as thousands see that his faith in God has withstood his scars to come through as refined as pure gold.

Michael decided to make another choice besides crawling off the altar. When the heat turned up, he determined to be a sweet-smelling sacrifice to God, just as Jesus had been (Eph. 5:2). As the prophet Samuel said, "To obey is better than sacrifice, and to heed is better than the fat of rams" (1 Sam. 15:22 NIV).

═══

Turning Point: When the heat of problems and pain burns into our very souls, we can crawl away and hide when it gets too hot, or we can choose to be living sacrifices who stay on the altar for His sake.

═══

When Jesus washed His disciples' feet, He set the perfect example of obedience for all of us. John must have remembered that night as he wrote one of his epistles and said, "Whoever says that he lives in God must live as Jesus lived" (1 John 2:6 NCV).

When I was younger, I thought I knew all about the foot-washing scene in John's Gospel. The truth is, I had much to learn about what it really means for my life. Instead of living as Jesus lived, I quietly decided to live as I wanted to live, but, of course, I would still try to be a very respectable and obedient Christian. After all, I was simply trying to protect myself from being hurt. *Who could really blame me for that?* I thought.

THE ALTAR NEVER COOLS FOR JONI

Mention Joni Eareckson Tada's name to believers in almost any country of the world, and smiles will break out everywhere. We all love her so much and know well the story of the beautiful and promising young athlete whose spinal column was severed in a diving accident.

We've probably all seen Joni's movie and read her books. We know that at one time she wished she could die because she couldn't deal with being handicapped. She even tried to persuade her friends to give her enough pills to end it all.

We marveled with Joni at the prospect of not being able to blow our own noses, comb our own hair, or reach out and touch someone. And through it all, Joni has become our hero.

In Pat Robertson's dressing room at the *700 Club* hangs a beautiful picture drawn by Joni, a verse of Scripture that she has illustrated. She's a gifted artist, a wonderful writer, and a beautiful singer. For many of us, the book is closed. She had a terrible accident; she struggled with her faith; she triumphed; now she is living happily ever after.

Not so. I've spent time with Joni throughout the years, and each time I realize that her story lives on every single day. It takes her almost two hours to get ready every morning. For years she has lived in a wheelchair, unable to do anything for herself.

Joni is very honest and very candid; she also has a great sense of humor. But along with all that, she has the desires of any woman. In the evening when her husband comes home after a busy day of teaching high school, she longs to be able to get up and throw her arms around his neck and say, "Welcome home! What kind of day have you had?"

Joni longs to be able to set a candlelit table, to do all the little things that we love to be able to do for one another, but she'll never be able to do them.

WE ALWAYS HOPE THE LORD WILL HURRY UP

We Christians say that we are willing to learn lessons from God, but our attitude really says, "Hurry up, Lord, and get on with it. I need to get this over with. If You have to teach me something that will help me to be a better Christian, okay. But if you could do it before lunchtime, I'd be very grateful, because I really do have a hectic schedule."

During the long days, weeks, months, and years of being immobile following her accident, Joni had plenty of time for the Lord's lessons. She learned to live day in and day out, year after year with the reality of a broken body. Even though she was paralyzed, in her heart Joni could have crawled off the altar as quickly as anyone else had she chosen to do so.

Joni could have given up on God. She could have raged at Him for the rest of her life, for allowing that horrific accident to happen. She could have listened to Satan's subtle promptings to feel sorry for herself. Instead, she chose to be a living sacrifice, and she continues to make that choice daily. Every time she wakes up, her body reminds her that it's another day that she has to make a choice—one more day to love God; one more day to trust Him.

It would be so much easier if life were like a game of riddles in which God gives us hints about the right questions to ask. Then we could solve our problems and move on. But life is not a game. It's really a worship service, and each of us is a living sacrifice.

Every time I think of Joni Eareckson Tada, I strengthen my resolve to stay on the altar for the right reasons. So did our friend Job.

THE ALTAR NEVER COOLED FOR JOB

Look back at Job. He certainly felt the heat of his altar. He began his long discourse with his friends by crying out, "Let the day of my birth be cursed" (Job 3:2 TLB). Don't we all feel this way sometimes?

"Why didn't I die at birth?" he went on. "Then I would be quiet now, asleep and at rest" (3:11, 13).

And finally he asked the question, "Why is a man allowed to be born if God is only going to give him a hopeless life of uselessness and frustration?" (3:23)

Job's altar was burning hot. Not long after that he cried out, "Oh, that God would grant the thing I long for most—to die beneath his hand, and be freed from his painful grip" (6:8–9).

Note that Job didn't contemplate suicide, as some do today. He didn't go to a Dr. Death to relieve himself of his pain. And we can only imagine the pain he endured by his description of himself: "My skin is filled with worms and blackness. My flesh breaks open, full of pus. My life flies by—day after hopeless day" (7:5–6).

Job remained on the altar for thirty-seven more chapters of Scripture, and goodness knows the time frame those chapters represent, since the Scripture does not give us a clue as to the amount of time that is passing.

Why do you suppose Job stayed on the altar? Halfway through his experience, covered with boils, and overwhelmed by the accusations of his friends, Job still said, "I know that my Redeemer lives, and that he will stand upon the earth at last. And I know that after this body has decayed, this body shall see God! Then he will be on my side!" (19:25–27).

Job and Joni are not the only Christians who choose to stay on the altar. Many contemporary Christians who are less well known than Joni have remained on the altar and endured disasters that could have broken them, people like Kathy Bartalsky.

MADE READY BY SUFFERING

Kathy and Steve Bartalsky felt called to the mission field. Steve was a helicopter pilot and had been accepted to work in Camaroon with Helimission, a group that reaches otherwise inaccessible areas and tribes with the gospel and medical supplies. Steve and Kathy had a brand-new baby girl, and friends and family warned them to wait until she was older to go overseas. But the Bartalskys believed their little one would be fine.

Just before they were to leave for Camaroon, Steve and Kathy's baby was diagnosed with spinal meningitis. She died when she was three months old.

The Bartalskys postponed their trip while they grieved their loss. As they were recovering, their desire to serve grew stronger than ever. At last they adopted a boy, Colby, and the three of them left for Camaroon.

Helimission has a unique and focused vision. Poisonous gas killed 1,700 people at Lake Nyof during 1986, and the

Helimission team was able to fly out the survivors. After the village people had reestablished themselves in the area, the Helimission pilots flew in 65 Bible students and 1,346 people gave their lives to Christ.

Steve and Kathy knew they were in the center of God's will for their lives by participating in the mission. Despite tough times, they had the unmistakable peace that comes from being where they should be.

Steve flew supplies into Uganda one day. To get there, he left from the capital of Camaroon, which was six hours from the village where Steve and Kathy lived. Steve and Kathy had decided that Kathy would leave Colby with a friend and then drive to the capital to pick up Steve when he returned.

Kathy did as planned and was there to hug Steve as he stepped onto the tarmac. The couple went inside for a cold drink before the long drive home. Just before they left, they received a telephone call.

Colby had accidentally drunk some poison. He was dead.

Kathy and Steve drove home in shocked silence.

A day later, Kathy and Steve buried their second child—this time in a foreign grave.

Kathy questioned God in agony. "Why would You do this to us a second time? We are here because You called us. Where is the sense in all this suffering?" She thought of the verse in Psalms that promised that those who honored God would live to see their children around their table. *What could it mean?* she wondered, for there she and Steve sat alone, two children dead before they were.

Kathy's sufferings drove her to look long and hard into the face of God to see if He was still a loving God. As she looked and questioned, God showed her a new level of love and gave her a new passion to serve Him, no matter what the cost.

Two months later Steve and Kathy moved to Addis Ababa in Ethiopia to fly famine relief. They forgot their own pain as they strove to help meet the needs and relieve the devastation of the people in the area. But tragedy soon visited the couple again.

Only three months after Steve and Kathy had settled in Addis Ababa, a group of men came to Kathy's door. One stepped forward.

"Kathy—it's Steve." All of the men looked solemn as the spokesman continued. "His helicopter crashed today when he went out, Kathy. There wasn't anything we could have done. He's . . . Steve's dead."

"Every time I thought I had given it all to Him," Kathy told me as she recounted the events, "I found there was more to give."

Her words reminded me of Paul's letter to the Philippians: "Yet indeed I also count all things loss for the excellence of the knowledge of Christ Jesus my Lord, for whom I have suffered the loss of all things, and count them as rubbish, that I may gain Christ and be found in Him . . . that I may know Him and the power of His resurrection, and the fellowship of His sufferings, being conformed to His death, if, by any means, I may attain to the resurrection from the dead" (Phil. 3:8–11 NKJV). Paul lost everything; yet, he felt his losses were rubbish—literally, from the Greek, *dung*—compared with the gain of Christ Jesus.

Paul longed more to know Christ and to be a partner with Christ in His pain than he did to hang on to his status or his righteousness that came from keeping the law. Kathy's longing to know Christ was greater than her desire to hang on to her two children and husband or to have them somehow brought back. She allowed herself to become a partner in Christ's sufferings through her grief. And she pressed on as Paul did: "Forgetting those things which are behind and reaching forward to those things which are ahead, I press toward the goal for the prize of the upward call of God in Christ Jesus" (Phil. 3:13–14 NKJV).

Kathy had Steve's friends take her to the site where his helicopter had crashed. There, at the clearing in the woods where her husband's mangled machinery lay, Kathy felt as if she were on holy ground. Steve had gone home to victory in that clearing. Kathy wanted to take off her shoes.

"If we believe in God only for the blessing He can give us," Kathy told me, "our belief in Him is not based on love and trust but on our own selfish desires and our own concept of what we think God owes us."

Kathy is happy. She is still young and attractive; pain has not hardened her. But when I look at Kathy, I feel as if the frivolity of life has been stripped away from her. She has left behind many of the things that don't matter and is clinging to the best God has to give—Himself.

Knowing Kathy has helped me believe for the first time that we can be glad when we suffer because it makes us ready for what really matters and what will last forever.

6

BE GOD'S FRIEND,
NOT JUST HIS SERVANT

===

Christian service is a poor substitute for Jesus Himself.
We must ask, "Do I want to run myself ragged doing
things for God, or do I want the best part—being His
friend and knowing Him face-to-face?"

I'm sorry, Sheila, but you're going to have to forget this concert tour. You have a growth on
your left vocal cord. You not only shouldn't be
singing, but you shouldn't even talk for a while."

In the spring of 1984, while I was still living in England,
London's leading throat specialist started putting away his
instruments while I sat there—stunned. The pain in my
throat had started about ten days before. I had gone to my
regular doctor, who gave me some antibiotics that he said
would take care of the problem. But they hadn't taken care
of the problem; in fact, my throat had become much worse.

Next I had prayed with leaders in our church for healing.

While I had never been the type who needed a miracle a day before breakfast, I did believe a hundred percent that I would be healed. This particular tour was just too important for me to let Satan win. In fact, after the prayer session, I went out into our garden and marched up and down, thanking God for everything He had ever done, including my healing. But afterward, I sounded more like a hoarse cat than ever.

With the tour due to start in just a couple of days, I made an appointment with the top throat specialist in London, hoping that he could give me a wonder pill or maybe a shot that would somehow make it possible for me to sing.

Now I sat there in shock and disbelief. I had come for a saving reprieve, not a sentence of doom. Didn't the doctor understand that twenty-five thousand tickets had already been sold for the biggest Christian concert tour in Britain's history?

"How long must I go without singing or even talking?" I asked. "Are you absolutely sure I can't do the tour?"

"Absolutely!" he said with the clipped firmness that specialists seem to favor. "You are not to sing or even speak for at least thirty days. Then we'll see. I may as well tell you that it's possible I'll have to operate, and you may never sing again."

HOW COULD THIS TOUR BE OFF?

I left the doctor's office and stepped onto a busy London sidewalk on one of those unusually bright sunny days that occasionally happen in May. The brilliant sunshine seemed to mock my somber mood. Somber? It was closer to total despair. How could I tell my manager and road crew that the tour was off? They had spent countless hours putting it all together, and we were so sure that God's hand was on every step.

The previous year I had become the host of the *Rock Gospel Show*, a thirty-minute program that aired once a week to about four million viewers. Because of BBC policy, I couldn't say a lot about my personal faith, but even playing Christian songs and making brief comments had people writing in to ask for more about the God I was talking about. Who was this Jesus? How could they know Him?

My manager and I had wondered how I could reach these people, and then the idea came to us: a gospel megatour of all Britain, in the biggest theaters in every good-sized community. The whole thing had gone beautifully—until now. Most of the theaters were sold out, but all concerts would have to be canceled. I took the train back to the suburbs, and my manager met me at the station. "Did he give you something?" was his immediate question. "Did he give you a spray or something for the pain?"

Following doctor's orders, I started writing something on a piece of paper. He had told me, "The minute you leave this room, I don't want you to say a thing. Use this pad and pencil from now on."

So my first note to my manager said, "You have to cancel the tour."

He looked at me in total disbelief. "What do you mean, I have to cancel the tour?"

I saw that I could never write fast enough to answer all his questions, so I decided I would break the doctor's rule just this once.

"Okay, I'm going to talk to you now, but this will be it. The doctor told me I have a growth on my vocal cords, and

I can't speak, much less sing, for a month. I might have to have an operation, and it's even possible I'll never be able to sing again. I can't say anymore to you now. You just need to know that you have to cancel the tour, and I'm so sorry."

When I arrived home, it seemed as if a black cloud had moved in from the sea and descended upon my head. At the same time my manager went up to his office and began making phone calls to the band and the promoters—and to the insurance company to find out if the tour was covered to make up for all our losses.

As soon as the news got out, phone calls started coming in, especially from band members' wives. One woman I had always looked up to said, "I believe that God has done this to you because you're getting too locked into who you are— you've taken God off the throne, so He has to shut you up."

Then another woman called and said, "Look, Sheila, we just have to have enough faith. If you and I have enough faith, this tour can still go ahead." This kind of pressure was just too much. Again I broke my doctor's rule and talked in a low whisper, telling her, "Look, I've prayed. I've asked for healing, and it hasn't happened. The doctor says there's a growth . . ."

My caller was like a Scottish terrier with her teeth in my leg—she just wouldn't let go. She kept saying, "Well, if you just have more faith, it will happen . . ."

I HAD TO GET ALONE WITH GOD

I realized I'd never be able to rest my voice in this kind of melee. I had to get away from well-meaning Christians and work all this out alone with God. My pastor helped me find people in our church who were willing to let me use their small vacation home on the south coast of England.

I packed a bag with a few things and took my dog, Tilly, who would be my only companion during ten days of prayer and fasting at the little beach house. (Tilly was the only one I wanted to see during this time because she wagged her tail whether I sang or not.)

Soon I was alone and, like Job, my first question was "Why?" I just couldn't understand. Didn't God realize what a big celebration He could have had in heaven after the tour was over and all those people had become Christians? What was going on? Were the band members' wives right? Did I think too much of myself? Didn't I have enough faith to trust God for healing?

For ten days I prayed, fasted, walked the beach, and asked God why. I tried to examine my life, and I kept wondering about those ominous words: *You may never sing again.* Is this what God had in mind? Singing had been my life. Ever since I graduated from London Bible College, one of my main goals had been to glorify God with my voice. I had served with British Youth for Christ. I had made records and done tours of Europe and America. I had sung everywhere, from giant cathedrals in Europe to tiny churches on the back roads of Kansas.

And now it was all over?

I had to wrestle with wondering whether I loved my singing ministry more than I loved Jesus Himself. After ten days of fasting and praying, I still had no answers.

On the last morning of my stay, I went back out on the beach near the cottage. As I watched the gentle waves roll in, I became aware of a blanket of God's love. I had run out of things to say, just as Job finally did.

His litany of ifs continued for one entire chapter (Job 31). He rehearsed all the ifs his friends had accused him of: "If I have lied and deceived . . . If I have longed for another man's wife . . . if I have been unfair to my servants . . . if I have hurt the poor or caused widows to weep, or refused food to hungry orphans . . . if I have put my trust in money . . . if I have rejoiced at harm to an enemy . . . let the Almighty show me that I am wrong" (TLB).

As I prayed that morning on the beach, I said to God, "Okay, I give up. If it's true that I love my career more than I love You, that I'm on some kind of ego trip, then please take it all away. *Don't give my voice back to me.*"

Until then I had never been willing to actually tell God I didn't need my voice back. But once I got the words out, it made all the difference. In the next few moments I got the distinct impression that God was saying, "Sheila, don't you understand that I love you because of who you are and not for what you do? Your security has been all wrapped up in thinking of yourself as Sheila Walsh the singer, the evangelist, the speaker, the person who goes out there and does it all for Me. But that's not why I love you. If you never sing another note, it will not matter to Me. I don't need you to do things for Me. I just really love you."

―――――

Turning Point: Christian service is a poor substitute for Jesus Himself. We must ask, "Do I want to run myself ragged doing things for God or do I want the best part—being His friend and knowing Him face-to-face?"

―――――

As I stood there on the beach, vulnerable and empty-handed, I realized that at that moment I was richer than I'd ever dreamed. Christian service is a poor substitute for Jesus Himself. We must ask whether we want to run ourselves ragged doing things for God, or do we want the best part: being His friend.

GOD HAS MANY SERVANTS
BUT FEW FRIENDS

Out of my ten days of walking the beach, that was the only answer God gave me, but it was enough. I realized that for God there is a giant difference between servanthood and friendship. On the night before He died on the cross, Jesus told His disciples that He didn't want to call them servants. He wanted to call them friends because He had made known to them everything He had heard from His heavenly Father (John 15:14–15).

Through that verse I could hear God telling me, "Sheila, I have many servants, but few friends. I have many people going places for Me, doing things for Me, but few who just love Me."

That thought burned into my heart and mind, and I determined to be one of God's friends, no matter what the cost.

It struck me that I had never asked God whether He wanted me to do the tour. I guess we had thought it would be sort of a surprise party for Him. Now I understood that God was not interested in having me run around doing things for Him. He was interested in my friendship, my love, and my companionship.

To this day, I still don't understand everything about what happened. I don't understand why things went wrong and why some people were hurt because of the tour's cancellation. But one lasting impression has never faded: If I never made another album, if I never sang another song, if I were no longer "hot on the Christian charts," it didn't matter. All that mattered was who I was to Jesus. That day I remembered something my mum had told me when I was just a young girl: "Who you are alone with Jesus—*that's who you really are.*"

That is so true for all of us. Who we are with Jesus Christ, our Savior and Friend, is who we really are. The public image doesn't matter. Who are we when we're alone with the Lord? The rest is empty rhetoric.

"SHEILA, YOUR THROAT IS HEALED"

A couple of days after getting home, I reported back to my doctor as he had suggested. It had been just over two weeks since he had warned me not to talk. He took X rays and, after looking at them, he turned to me with a puzzled expression. "Sheila, the growth is gone. It just isn't there anymore. I still suggest you go easy on talking for another week or two, but it looks as if your throat is healed."

I went home on cloud nine and sat down to put my feelings and thoughts into a song of some kind. Over the next few days, I started thinking about how trapeze performers start out needing a safety net. Later they become more confident, and the net is taken away. It was a spiritual picture of what I had done with my life. I had decided that I was far enough along to go it on my own, and I didn't need the safety net anymore. God had given me back my voice, but He had left me with a gentle warning.

Serving God is important, even vital, but it should never come ahead of realizing that He is first of all our Friend, and without His friendship, life is an empty treadmill. Christianity is not an employer-employee contract; it is a relationship between a loving heavenly Father and His children.

JOB: GOD'S SERVANT AND FRIEND

In the opening scenes of the story of Job, Satan accused Job of being God's servile employee because Job was getting a good deal. God disagreed, and this confrontation led to a great cosmic struggle between good and evil, played out in the life of one man.

Job's response to incredible disaster, pain, and suffering proves that he was more than simply a servant who had been living a righteous life because it paid off. After Satan's first attack, Job still saw God as his Friend. He still said, "The LORD gave these things to me, and he has taken them away. Praise the name of the Lord" (Job 1:21 NCV).

Still later in the story, as Job was in the midst of his debates with his three friends, who tried to convince him that his sins had caused his suffering, Job admitted that he had a strong complaint because God's hand seemed to be heavy against him. He wanted to find God to present his case to Him. He knew that God would listen. Job said:

> But God knows the way that I take,
> and when he has tested me,
> I will come out like gold.

My feet have closely followed his steps;
I have stayed in his way;
I did not turn aside.
I have never left the commands he has spoken.
I have treasured his words more than my own (23:10–12).

Again and again in Job's story, we see that there is more between him and God than an employer-employee relationship. He was God's servant, true, but he was also God's friend. Throughout his entire ordeal, Job's reactions prove that he did not serve God for what he could get out of Him but for what he could give to Him from the very core of his being. Job did not serve God out of fear or duty. He served God out of love, and so it should be between friends.

At times it is easy for us to get caught up in Christian "service." We can become members of every committee and attend every prayer group. Wherever there is a job to be done in the church, we will be there. We may run ourselves ragged doing things for God and lose Him in the midst of it all. Ultimately, only our loyalty to Him as a person and a friend will hold us when life is tough. That's what I've learned, and so have a number of Christians I've met.

DAVE BOYER ASKED HIS FRIEND FOR HELP

I had never met Dave Boyer when he got up to sing at a banquet I was attending. I'd heard him sing a couple of times, but what he did that evening was remarkable. He began to share, not just the successes and the good things, but the struggles he had had in his life.

Many people present who knew Dave were aware of his

story. Before he had ever come to the Lord, he had been in real trouble. But as he talked to us that night, he told us of his second struggle. After he had come to the Lord, he had battled the very things that had threatened to tear him apart before his conversion.

I was so impressed with Dave that evening that I invited him to be my guest on *Heart to Heart.* Dave graciously agreed to come and share his story.

A few weeks later he was with us in Virginia Beach. When I interviewed him on the program, I was struck by how humble and genuine he was as he shared with our viewers the kind of life he had led before he knew Jesus—and what happened later when he began to slip.

Dave grew up in a godly home and was active in the church his father pastored, singing in the choir and regularly attending other functions. He never took his relationship with Jesus seriously, however, and at age fifteen he began pursuing a career as a professional singer and entertainer.

By the age of eighteen he took the stage name "Joey Stevens" and began emceeing at the 500 Club in Atlantic City, where stars like Frank Sinatra, Dean Martin, Jerry Lewis, and Sammy Davis Jr. became his heroes.

But the entire nightclub scene took its toll, and Dave's marriage began to suffer. He started drinking heavily and using drugs. At times he was abusive to his wife and daughter, and he and his wife finally separated.

Dave knew that deep inside something was very wrong, but he seemed powerless to deal with it. His father, a very godly man, had been very important in his life. As Dave struggled amid all of his problems, his father died. Something snapped deep inside Dave.

Dave found himself, late at night, walking toward the railroad tracks, where he planned to wait for a train to come and end his life. A small Methodist church he passed on the way brought back a flood of memories of his father's church. In despair, Dave fell on the church steps, ramming his head against the door and crying, "God, let me live for You—give me the strength somehow." In that moment of desperation, Dave somehow realized that God did love him as He loved all people, and Dave had a fleeting moment of feeling peace and security.

Dave made his way to a telephone and called his brother, who was pastoring their late father's church. They arranged to meet, and after praying for several hours with his brother, Dave committed his life to Jesus Christ for the first time.

God proceeded to do many miracles in his life. His dependence on drugs and alcohol ended. He was reunited with his wife and daughter, and together they began building a Christ-centered home.

To show his gratitude, Dave began to sing for the Lord and was soon Christian music's number-one big-band-style vocalist. Bookings poured in, and his schedule became extremely busy. He found himself, like many of us do, worn out from traveling the Christian circuit. He seldom had a chance to sit down on Sundays in his own fellowship and receive spiritual nurture and support. Instead he was always out somewhere else, helping to provide for everyone else.

Slowly, just a little at a time, Dave began drinking again. He turned away from his real Friend and began to rely on a comfortable old friend, which was no friend at all.

One night a pastor sat down with Dave and asked, "Dave, how are you doing?"

Dave responded with the usual answer we all give when we want to cover up what's really going on inside: "Hey, I'm doing fine, brother, thank you."

"No, Dave," his friend replied. "Now really, how are you doing?"

Dave could see he was at the end of the line, and so he opened up and cried out for help. At that moment God moved in and caught him before he fell completely. Just as his fingers were slipping, just as his grip was failing, the bigger, stronger hand of God caught him and would not let him fall.

WE CAN'T EARN GOD'S FRIENDSHIP

As I listened to Dave tell his story, so many things were going through my mind. I thought of other people in responsible positions—pastors, teachers, leaders—who so desperately need help but are unable to reach out and say, "Please help me! I'm in real trouble."

Too many Christians are enslaved by their own ministries, trapped into thinking they can't be real, honest, or open because that would undermine their testimony—and their status.

I marveled at how wonderful it was when Dave was able to reach out and ask for the help he needed. His story made me realize again that ministry *is* a poor substitute for Jesus' friendship.

As the broadcast ended, Dave stood up and began to sing "Calvary Covers It All." I sat in the quietness of the studio and wept in gratitude for the fact that when we blow it, when we fall flat on our faces, when we try and don't make it, *there is still a place to go.* Whether you are nine or ninety, whether you have known the Lord for two weeks or twenty years, you can always say to Him, "Why did I walk away? You were my life. You patiently taught me how to fly, and that was my big mistake. I thought I could fly on my own. But that isn't so. Please hold me tight. *Don't let me go!*"

That's what I was saying to God that day on the beach, when I faced the possibility of never singing again. I was asking Jesus for help. I knew I couldn't make it on my own. London's finest throat specialist had told me I might never sing again. But even more important at that moment, I didn't want to make it on my own. Whatever God had for me was fine. And just being His friend would be enough.

7

KEEPING IT SIMPLE
KEEPS IT REAL

When this complex, plastic world tries to squeeze us into a designer mold, we can let pride take over, or we can shake free to live the simple truth of the gospel with humility.

*I*t happened on the freeway, just a few weeks after I started cohosting the *700 Club* in 1987. I suppose you could say my integrity got slapped in the face and, to tell the truth, I needed it!

I flipped on the radio, hoping for a little lift from one of the local Christian stations, and a familiar song filled the car. The vocalist was someone I knew well in the Christian music industry. There had been a day when that song would have given me what I was looking for. I used to play it while doing housework and, instead of feeling drowned in drudgery, I'd wind up having a ball. But on this particular evening, the song didn't do a thing for me.

The lyrics didn't come close to what I was feeling and where I was hurting, especially for other people. After being on the *700 Club* for just a few weeks, I had new sensitivity to what was happening in the world and how badly people needed a healing touch from Christ.

MY FRIENDS TOLD ME I WAS SELLING OUT

When I had told my friends that I was praying about Pat Robertson's invitation to become cohost for the *700 Club,* some of them replied, "If you take that job, you'll bury your head in Christian television, and you'll never breathe clean air again. You'll wind up sheltering yourself from the real world. You're selling out to the 'Blue Rinse Brigade'!"

But a funny thing had happened to me on my way to irrelevancy. From the very first week, cohosting the *700 Club* broadcasts was like having God throw a bucket of ice water in my face every morning. I realized that, while I had thought I knew about needs and hurts, I didn't really know much at all.

I'd given plenty of Christian concerts and even counseled people afterward, but now it seemed that I had been singing happy little Christian songs for nice Christian people. We'd all have fun and then go home feeling, "Wow! We've really met some needs tonight."

I'm sure we did meet some needs, but now I became aware of so many more. Daily I was dealing with people who had been brought up in desperate poverty, people caught in the trap of prostitution, drug addiction, child abuse, and myriad other human tragedies.

I had been so busy during those first few weeks that I

hadn't realized how much I was changing. Now one song on the radio brought it all home. I actually pulled the car off on an emergency parking space and sat there thinking, *What on earth have I been doing all this time? All these people are out there with real, open wounds, and so much of what I did was like blowing up balloons and saying, "Yippee! Let's all love Jesus!"*

I'M TIRED OF BEING A HAMSTER

Later, I thought, *I'm not even sure I want to make another album. I don't want to be a hamster on a treadmill. Every year I turn out an album and do a tour because it's expected. If what I sing really doesn't make a difference, I'm not sure I want to do it anymore.*

I decided to contact Dan Posthuma, who was head of the Myrrh label at Word Records, the division that recorded my albums. By the next day, however, I was caught up in the intense routine at the *700 Club*, and I forgot about making the call.

Less than ten days later, however, Dan Posthuma called me. "Sheila, it's about that time again. What's your thinking for a new album?"

I shared with Dan what had happened to me, and then I added, "You know, Dan, I'm not sure I want to do another album. I don't know where I am anymore in this whole thing."

Instead of getting angry or pressuring me to produce another product, Dan said, "I understand. Why don't we get together and talk about this? Greg Nelson has expressed some interest in doing something."

Greg Nelson is one of the top producers in the country and has done albums for people like Sandi Patti and Steve Green. I flew down to Nashville to talk with Greg. I told him what had been going on with me. As I shared my story with him, his eyes filled with tears. "Sheila," he said, "I agree with you with all my heart. I don't want to just turn out another record. I want to make a difference."

We decided to get together for a brainstorming weekend—Dan, Greg, my manager Steve Lorenz, and me. We chose Dallas, somewhat of a midway point for all of us.

I prepared for that weekend by writing down the subjects that I had been thinking a great deal about recently. I wanted to sing about what it's like to be alone, what it's like to be disillusioned and to have all your dreams crumble around you. Was there any good news I could bring to people? Was there anything I could take to the streets, to the living rooms, to the concert stage that would make sense the way Jesus made sense when He spoke to His listeners' deepest needs?

We checked in at the hotel in Dallas and had a weekend-long "listening party." Whenever you are thinking about doing a new album, you put out the word, and songwriters send in their latest efforts. Dan brought some great new songs that had come in for his consideration, and Greg brought others as well. We had dozens of songs to sort out as we listened, talked, and prayed. As the hours went by, we identified the things we thought were important. We were looking for a plumb line—ten issues or subjects that would communicate the truth of the gospel.

Over that weekend, we heard many really great songs. We knew that a lot of them would get plenty of air play, but if they didn't say what we wanted the album to say, we declined to do them. Every song had to speak the simple truth, the kind of truth that touches the soul and takes root in your heart.

We wanted every one of these songs to be a lasting one, something that would communicate the Word of God, which the writer of Hebrews says is living and active and sharper than any two-edged sword (Heb. 4:12).

It was a tough weekend because we had to balance our need to be artistic, creative, and poetic with what we felt was more important—the need to be real, helpful, and true to the simple truth of the gospel. We had to decide how much we valued our integrity as musicians and entertainers against how much we valued our integrity as servants of Christ.

FROM SAND TO SOLID ROCK

For my *Shadow Lands* album, which had come out several years before, I had recorded several songs that spoke of Christ, but in the commercial pop rock vein. The album was fairly successful, and it got great reviews in many different Christian magazines, which said I was on the "radical cutting edge of Christian rock music."

Typical of the songs in the album was "Sand in the Hand," which included these lyrics:

> Love is a miracle, a vision to see
> Sand in the hand will run away
> But love in the heart will stay
> Sand in the hand will run away, run away.
> It's not just a dream, love is forevermore and ever green.[1]

Not exactly *War and Peace*, but the kind of stuff that kids love to repeat without doing much thinking.

For our new album, however, we wrote songs like "Come into His Kingdom." A few lines of that song show the difference:

> Another morning comes, you give yourself away
> To a million things that take your time
> You lose another day.
> Your dreams can fall apart and cry out in despair
> You built your world so carefully and no one seems to
>   care.
> But there's a place for travel-worn and weary ones
> You can leave your dusty shoes outside the door.
> For when you come into His Kingdom
> You're going to find love
> Find that you've just begun
> When you come into His Kingdom, no matter who, no
>   matter what you've done.[2]

We Settled on Simple Truth

The result of our weekend together was an album, appropriately titled *Simple Truth*. Its ten songs spoke of God's calling of love, losing your life so you can find it, being there for others, quiet times with God, and giving Him all the glory. We even included the old hymn "Savior, Like a Shepherd Lead Us" because it so clearly stated the simple walk of the committed Christian.

The first time I performed songs from *Simple Truth* in concert was at the Billy Graham Crusade in London in 1989, which was broadcast by satellite across Great Britain. A few days later, I received a letter from a woman in northern England, whose brother had attended the meeting and heard me sing "God Loves You." A medical doctor, he had never been particularly interested in the claims of the gospel before, but as he heard the words of the song he felt God's presence in a new and different way and realized for the very first time that God did love him. Even before Dr. Graham preached, this man had made up his mind from hearing my song. He went forward and gave his life to Christ.

Another letter, from a young woman who had had an abortion, told me of how she had been a Christian, but life had closed in upon her. She thought she had no choice but to kill the child in her womb, and she had lived in a nightmare of guilt ever since. She bought *Simple Truth*, and when she heard "God Loves You," she realized that God had forgiven her and that she could at last forgive herself.

Letters like these are far more meaningful to me than favorable reviews, lots of air play, or even big sales. *Simple Truth* was our team effort to do away with plastic, designer-suit Christianity and go for the real thing. Ever since the televangelist scandals broke in headlines and over TV newscasts in the mid 80s, Christian integrity has been under greater scrutiny and criticism than ever. I clearly remember where I was and what I was doing when the sad news of Jim Bakker's private life hit the headlines.

IT WAS LIKE A SOAP OPERA, BUT WORSE

I had crawled out of bed and was having some breakfast when I flipped on the news and was greeted with a report that stunned me. I knew Jim and Tammy Bakker and had made several appearances on their *PTL* show. Disbelief washed across me in huge waves as I heard the lurid details that sounded like a soap opera out of control. The ill-disguised delight on the face of the cynical TV reporter was a sign of what was to come in media coverage during the following weeks and months. One more evangelical figurehead was being toppled, and I could tell this reporter was relishing his work.

I needed to get out into the fresh air, to think and pray. I felt bombarded by mixed emotions: anger, sorrow, disappointment, but, most of all, sadness.

I found myself outside a favorite little French café a few blocks from where I was living in Laguna Beach. As I sat on the patio with the steam of cappuccino competing with the heat of the day, I began to write the lyrics to a song on a table napkin with a borrowed pencil.

Up until then, I had done little or no writing of my own songs. But for some reason, that morning it seemed easy for me to express my heart, and the words to "It Could Have Been Me" flowed out. Another fragile Christian warrior had indeed slipped. He had fallen from grace, and now the vultures were circling.

So much of our Christian heritage seems to be built on a pyramid system. The person at the top has a long way to fall, and many delight in kicking him or her on the way down.

Why are we so cruel to one another? Why do we lash out so violently when someone crumbles? I'm not saying that sin should not be dealt with—far from it. I believe with all my heart in discipline within the body of Christ. I guess I'm referring to the spectators who cheer as the blade falls, who find it so much easier to believe the worst than to hold on to the best. Perhaps we hit out most strongly at those who live out our private temptations. As I said in "It Could Have Been Me,"

> And in our hearts we fear
> The ones whose lives are like our own
> Whose shadows dance like demons in our minds.[3]

Two ideas motivated me as I put down the words for the song on that napkin. Already I was looking ahead to the months of endless headlines and news angles. I could picture the ridicule and scorn that would be heaped upon the church as a whole, for surely this kind of tragedy would be a late-night talk show host's dream.

But even more important, as I thought of Jim and Tammy Bakker fielding reporters' cynical questions, I realized that in many ways it could have been me. Long before the *PTL* scandal broke, the Lord had been gently dealing with my overconfidence. I had always felt strong as a Christian, that with Jesus by my side I could go anywhere, do anything, withstand any pressure and temptation. I never realized the subtle trap of my naive pride.

IT COULD HAVE BEEN ME

I heard the news today that another soldier stumbled,
A fragile warrior slipped and fell from grace.
The vultures swooped to tear his heart
And pin him to the ground
And from the shadows someone took his place.

Today we'll talk amongst ourselves,
We never bought his words.
We'll say we saw the madness in his eye.
Tomorrow he's forgotten as we've scrubbed him from our
    hearts
And as he bleeds we slowly turn our eyes.

But it could have been me.
I could have been the one to lose my grip and fall.
It could have been me,
The one who takes such subtle pride in always standing
    tall.
For unless you hold me tightly, Lord, and I can hold on,
    too,
Then tomorrow in the news it could be me . . . [4]

Just as James and John asked Jesus if they could sit on His right and left in heaven, so also I wanted to be right up there with them. When the Lord asked whether they knew what they were saying, like pompous children they declared their suitability for the job. But history bears out that they were not able to stand when Jesus stood, not able to bleed when He bled. Only He is able. We never have been; we never will be. If we are truthful with ourselves, we must reject pride and self-reliance and admit that we are not able to stand without Jesus.

Without God's grace in our lives, then, truly it could be us. Our daily choices can make us or break us. This complex, plastic world can squeeze us into its designer mold, or we can strive to live the simple truths of the gospel with humility and love.

======

Turning Point: When this complex, plastic world tries to squeeze us into a designer mold, we can let pride take over, or we can shake free to live the simple truth of the gospel with humility.

======

I remember attending a convention at which Luis Palau, the Argentinean evangelist, was the main speaker. His theme was the well-known challenge from Jesus to "take up your cross and follow Me" (Matt. 16:24). As Palau held that challenge before us, we were faced with our lack of understanding. We like to cradle spiritual phrases, clutching them to our bosoms, but they are useless if there is no daily application in our lives.

Each day we have to make choices. Often they are not choices between extremes of good and evil where the answer is apparent. The answer seems to lie somewhere in the gray, and that is where we can quickly become tarnished.

WHEN SATAN IS MOST DANGEROUS

Working in a medium like television or on a Women of Faith tour leaves me highly visible—and very vulnerable. Weekly I learned that walking as Christ walked requires delicate balance. I meet many people who are asking, "Where are You, God? Are You really there, or is my faith just something I've built to form a crutch?" For many people, Satan is definitely there, perched on their backs, creating havoc and chaos of all kinds.

Satan can be subtle, and he's never more dangerous than

when you think you've made some progress as a Christian, that you've done something right and you "just know God is pleased." Since we all have the clay feet of fallibility, it's important for us to have a healthy assessment of our weaknesses as well as our strengths. If we don't, we can wind up taking our eyes off Jesus and find ourselves in mud. Back in 1990, when I was cohost of the *700 Club*, I learned again that Christian living isn't putting notches on your spiritual gun; it's walking the way of the pilgrim. Sometimes you move forward at a good pace, and other times you make choices that force you to slip back.

CINDY WAS DYING OF LEUKEMIA

It was early November and well past 6:00 in the evening. It had been a long day, during which I had taped four shows for *Heart to Heart*. I was looking forward to a rare weekend at home—no traveling, no concerts, just kicking back to relax.

I was at my desk, picking up a few things for Monday's *700 Club*, when Laura, my secretary, stopped me.

"Sheila, we just got a call from one of our Founder members. He's a doctor in a children's hospital in Phoenix."

"Did he say what he wanted?" I asked, glancing at my watch.

"He has a young patient, a fourteen-year-old girl who is dying of leukemia. You're her favorite singer. She has your tape by her bed and listens to it all the time. She'd really like you to call."

"Do you have the hospital's number and the girl's name?"

Laura gave me the slip of paper, and as I looked at the name, Cindy, and the number, weariness flooded over me as I thought of what I might say to a dying girl when I was feeling so tired myself.

I looked at Laura, hoping she could see how weary I was and then said, "Maybe it could wait until Monday?"

Laura didn't say anything, but her raised eyebrows sent me a signal. I put the slip of paper in my purse and headed for the elevator. As I punched the button, I knew I had made the wrong decision. I turned around and hurried past Laura, saying, "I'm just going to go ahead and call this girl. I really think I should."

As I dialed the number, I asked God for help—and a lot of wisdom. What do you say to a fourteen-year-old girl who's dying? How do you comfort someone whose life force is being sucked way?

The call went through, and a tired voice answered, "Hello, can I help you?"

I swallowed quickly, "Yes, this is Sheila Walsh. I'm calling about Cindy."

"Oh, Sheila, I'm *so* glad you called. I'm Cindy's mother."

She told me how weak her daughter was and then went on; "She won't be able to talk. She's in a lot of pain. Please don't be distressed by her little moans. She really loves you, and she'll be so happy to hear your voice. I'm going to hold the phone to her ear."

Lord, help me, please. What do I say?

"Hi, Cindy, it's Sheila. I'm so sorry you're sick."

I talked for a while, telling Cindy that the Lord loved her and that I was praying for her. All I could hear were little sounds, almost like a tiny animal in distress. Then I began to read from a few of my favorite psalms, beginning with Psalm 91: "He who dwells in the shelter of the Most High will rest in the shadow of the Almighty . . . Surely He will save you from the fowler's snare and from the deadly pestilence" (NIV).

Next I turned to Psalm 139: "O LORD, you have searched me and you know me . . . you have laid your hand upon me . . . your hand will guide me, your right hand will hold me fast" (NIV).

And finally I read from Psalm 23, the familiar words taking on a new and poignant meaning at that moment: "The LORD is my shepherd, I shall not be in want . . . Even though I walk through the valley of the shadow of death, I will fear no evil, for you are here with me . . . Surely goodness and love will follow me . . . and I will dwell in the house of the LORD forever" (NIV).

I prayed with Cindy, and then her mom came back on the line: "Sheila, she's smiling. Thank you." I gave Cindy's mother my home phone number and told her to feel free to call me.

When I came back in on Monday morning, there was a message. Cindy was with the Lord. I sat at my desk and wept for her family. I felt so sad for the painful weeks and months that lay ahead: their first Christmas without her, her birthday, her friends growing into womanhood. For Cindy, there was no more pain. For those left behind, there would be many hard days.

In a few days I received a lovely letter from Cindy's doctor, who told me how much it had meant to Cindy and her mother that I had called. Cindy had attended my concert in Phoenix the year before. There had been no sign of leukemia then, but when it struck it had worked very rapidly to destroy her body.

Helping Cindy as she stood on the threshold of heaven was hard, but in a strange and wonderful way it was also good. It was one of those times I was sure I had been obedient to what God was telling me. As I lay in bed that night, I thought about how I had changed from being a presumptuous teenager who wanted God to give her all of Scotland. "Lord," I prayed, "I don't want to talk so much about great exploits. I just want to try to live them in small ways."

I fell asleep feeling good because I had done what God told me to do when He told me to do it. I forgot for a moment that I still had clay feet, but as I slept, it began to rain.

HOW CLAY FEET CAN SLIP IN A HURRY

Three weeks after I talked to Cindy, I found myself working late at the office again, this time on the night before Thanksgiving. I finished up my work for the day and looked at my watch. It was 5:30, and I told myself, "Okay, you're out of here." I grabbed my car keys and was headed for the door when Laura's familiar voice stopped me: "Sheila!"

As I turned, Laura said, "We've had a call from a young girl. Her name is Jennifer. She's eighteen, and she says she really needs to talk with you. I think she's in real trouble."

Oh, great! I muttered to myself. *She thinks she's in trouble! If I don't get out of here, I'll never find that leg of lamb for tomorrow's dinner.*

"Do you think I could wait for a couple of days before I call her?" I asked Laura.

"No, I really don't," Laura said. "The girl mentioned something about suicide."

I grabbed the slip of paper and with mixed emotions

headed down to my dressing room to make the call. One part of me was screaming, *You've got to get out of here. You're already late, and you've got stops to make on the way home.*

But another voice said, *If you don't call, it's going to ruin your Thanksgiving, and you're not going to enjoy that lamb. You'll feel guilty because you didn't make the call.*

I dialed the number, and as I waited for the connection, I struggled out of my shirt and skirt and tried to get into my jeans.

"Hello," said a very quiet voice.

"Hi, Jennifer? This is Sheila Walsh. I hear you wanted to talk to me."

I kicked my shoes into the closet and tried to reach for my sneakers, almost pulling the phone off the wall.

"Oh, thanks for calling. I didn't think you'd call."

"Well, yeah, Jennifer, of course I'd call you. I care. That's why I called you."

I knew those were the right words to say, but I didn't really feel them deep in my heart at that moment. Jennifer began talking about her life, which she thought was very unfair. It didn't take her long to start making statements that sounded unfair to everyone else as well. She had no friends, and nobody cared for her at all. No, she didn't go to church because nobody in any of the churches really loved her; besides, she loved God more than anybody else anyhow.

Jennifer went on like this for several minutes, and I began to get irritated. "How can you say you love God more than anybody else?" I said a bit crossly. "If you really loved God, it would make you more loving rather than just feeling sorry for yourself."

I was hoping that being a bit firm with Jennifer would

help. At least that's what I told myself, but what I was really saying was, "Hurry up and get better fast, because I've got to go out and buy this jolly leg of lamb and be ready for Thanksgiving."

Then I heard her say, "You know, I just called up to get you to pray for me." And she proceeded to quote the verse that we're always quoting on the *700 Club*: "I tell you that if two of you on earth agree about something and pray for it, it will be done for you by my Father in heaven" (Matt. 18:19).

"But, Jennifer, I'm not sure I can pray," I told her. "We can't pray together because we don't agree. You tell me you love God but that you've decided to take your own life. You're telling me you can look at the Cross and literally say to Jesus, 'Hey, You blew it. I'm not worth what You did when You died for me.' You're telling Jesus that He was wrong and that your only way out is to end it."

"Well," said Jennifer after a few seconds of silence, "I've got bulimia, and I'm going to die anyway, so what's the difference?"

I asked her to tell me about it, and her story poured out. Over the past three years, she had thrown up every day of her life. Her symptoms sounded like those of a true bulimic, straight down the line. Because of all her vomiting, the enamel on her teeth had dissolved. I was convinced that she was truly in a bad way. I also started feeling convicted about getting too firm with her.

We had talked for over twenty minutes when she said, "I'm going to have to go now because I'm meeting my mom, and if I'm late she'll get really angry. Everybody in my family gets angry. All there is in our house is anger. I didn't call wanting you to get angry with me. Why are you angry with me? I thought you would pray for me. I just need a friend. I should have known you were just like everybody else."

I became a bit irritated and protested, "Jennifer, I wouldn't have called if I were just like everybody else . . ."

My words were barely out of my mouth when I realized that Jennifer was right. I sat for a few moments in stunned silence, exposed, ugly, a fraud. I *had* been acting like everybody else. I had really blown it—big time blown it. Jennifer was ready to let go of everything, and I wasn't helping her much.

"Look, Jennifer, I'm really sorry. I know you're right. I have no right to get angry with you, and I'm really sorry. Do you still want me to pray for you?"

There was more silence, and then Jennifer finally said, "Yeah . . . I really would love for you to pray for me. I'm all alone."

After I prayed for Jennifer and we were saying our good-byes she said, "I'd love it if I could just call sometimes. I just want to know there is another way to live, and I know you're right. I know there's another way to live, but I just can't find it. I just can't get out of myself right now."

I Wasn't Mother Teresa After All

We hung up, and I got down on my knees and wept, sliding in the muddy mess my clay feet had left. I saw myself so clearly, and I asked God to forgive me for the anger and pride that made me try to fit Jennifer into a slot. To me, she had been problem "3A." I knew the solution to problem "3A," but Jennifer just wouldn't fit. She just wouldn't grab my pat answers quickly enough to let me get out there, to do all the things I had to do.

Talking to Jennifer slapped me in the face with my own humanity. I realized I hadn't become Mother Teresa overnight after all. I wanted to be the kind of person who could be there for people, but I knew that I was human just like everyone else. I'm not just "Sheila who's always waiting at the other end of the line at the *700 Club*." I have a home, and that night I wanted to get home and fix Thanksgiving dinner.

Sometimes the most loving thing God can do is to hold up a mirror before our faces and let us gaze at the stark reality of what we're really like. I hadn't been honest enough to say, "Laura, I'm tired, and I have several things to do before I go home. Can you get one of our phone counselors involved?" I guess I was afraid I would damage my good name as a "caring" person.

Neither had I been honest enough to say, "Lord, I don't want to make this call. I want to go home, but someone needs my help so I need Yours. Please give me Your love and help me to communicate it."

I had forgotten to pray. I had been in a hurry, and I thought I could handle this caller in just a few minutes and be on my way. I learned a good lesson that day. One of the keys to living the Christian life is to have healthy humility and to be ever aware of the dangers of subtle pride.

The minute we begin to believe our own publicity, we are in for a nasty slide. The moment we feel we are invincible, the enemy crawls through one of the cracks of our pride and delights in showing us otherwise. Pride can be so subtle. It always begins with lies—the little comforting lies that we tell ourselves: "You're not like everybody else. You're strong. It'll never happen to you."

The truth is that we are all flawed creatures, and if we crawl out from under the protective wing of the Lord, we are most vulnerable. As Joy Dawson, author and speaker, said, "There are no extraordinary Christians—only ordinary Christians who serve an extraordinary God."

As Christ built His church, He picked very ordinary people to be His disciples, and there was no better example of how ordinary a follower of Christ could be than Peter. When it came to clay feet, he wore size twelve and then some.

"LORD, I'LL NEVER FAIL YOU!"

Peter made the same mistake I had made. He bought into Satan's lie: "You're not like everybody else. You're strong. It'll never happen to you." We know the scene well. After eating their Passover supper, Jesus and His disciples were preparing to leave for the Mount of Olives, but Jesus paused to tell them, "Tonight you will all stumble in your faith on account of me." Then He quoted from the prophet Zechariah (13:7), saying, "I will kill the shepherd, and the sheep will scatter" (Matt. 26:31 NCV).

Peter, however, protested. He knew the Lord couldn't be referring to him! He interrupted Jesus, saying, "Everyone else may stumble in their faith because of you, but I will not" (v. 33).

Jesus fixed him with a knowing look: "I tell you the truth, tonight before the rooster crows you will say three times that you do not know me" (v. 34).

Peter responded. "I will never say that I don't know you!

I will even die with you!" (v. 35). And then the Gospel account adds an interesting sentence: "And all the other followers said the same thing."

Three hours later, Peter denied Christ. Not once. Not twice. But three times, just as Jesus had predicted.

Peter was no different from any of us. He needed the Lord's protective wing. There are no extraordinary Christians, even in the Bible. We all have feet of clay. We all falter when we succumb to the sin of pride.

Despite Peter's failures, Jesus gave him another chance, just as He does for you and me.

After the Resurrection, Jesus and Peter met face-to-face on the shores of the Sea of Galilee to take care of unfinished business. Jesus did not plan to humiliate Peter, but He did want him to know the difference between the humble trust that was now in his heart and the foolish pride that he had displayed the night before the Crucifixion.

Three times Jesus asked the same question: "Peter, do you love Me? Yes, I know you've blown it, and I know you're ashamed, but that's not what I'm asking, Peter. I want to know, do you love Me?"

Peter looked into the eyes of the Son of God, his guilt bathed in the sea of Jesus' overwhelming love, and said, "Lord, You know everything. You know that I love You!"

And the Lord answered, "Then take care of My sheep" (John 21:1–18).

When Peter heard his assignment from the Lord, he knew beyond any doubt that he had been forgiven. Now he was ready to walk closely in His Master's footsteps because he had a new understanding of why and how his feet were made of clay.

So it is with all of us. We're going to make mistakes. We do fall flat on our faces at times. We are fallible and flawed, but Christ is able and willing to restore us. If we love Him, if we truly love Him, He will save us from our pride.

The Lord used Jennifer to remind me of what can happen when I try to stand on my own two clay feet without His help. When the stormy days come with all their pressures, it's going to be a mess, and everybody is going to get covered with mud.

I was also reminded that the Christian's direction is always forward, but there are bound to be detours and some slipping back. Sometimes we think we've become something special, because God has given us grace enough to be there for some people and to see them helped, as Cindy was helped. And then, just as we begin to go off on a tangent and become satisfied with how incredible we are and how willing we are just to be there for everybody, we are suddenly brought up short. We realize that we're still selfish, and a leg of lamb can become more important than an eighteen-year-old who thinks she has nothing to live for.

8

WHEN ALL OF HEAVEN
IS SILENT

=====

When God seems far away and our prayers bounce off the ceiling, we can give in to despair, or we can keep going on to heaven in simple trust.

*B*efore the Women of Faith Conference in Charlotte in 1998, Barry's mom called me and said, "I went to the doctor, and my cancer cell count has doubled since the last time. He told me of a man in Charlotte named Mahesh Chavda. My doctor told me that this man has a remarkable healing ministry."

I was amazed. "I know this man," I said. "I interviewed him on the *700 Club* about seven years ago. We had a lot of people through the *700 Club* who had healing ministries. Of all the people, I related to Mahesh the most. There was nothing spectacular about his presentation; he was a very quiet, humble man. I loved him. Why don't we go?"

Eleanor agreed, so I called the church office and found

out the healing service was going to be on Friday night, which is the night I speak. I'm never through until 11:00. So I called back and they agreed that we could bring her after we finished. We arrived just as the service was ending.

It was really touching for me. Eleanor is my mother-in-law but she is also a sister in the Lord, a fellow pilgrim, someone who is struggling to know God in the midst of the pain in her life.

Barry couldn't talk. He just sat with his head in his hands and wept. I have only seen Barry cry a couple of times before. Once was when Christian was born. There is something about the gift of life and the reality of death and, of course, this is his mother.

Mahesh invited people to come to the front for prayer. Barry's mom went up to the altar, and Barry and I knelt behind her. Mahesh came up to us, but he didn't recognize me. Yet Mahesh spent a lot of time praying for Eleanor without knowing that she was my mother-in-law. He asked her what was wrong, he brought his elders over and anointed her with oil, and then they blew the shofar trumpets, which have been blown since the beginning of Jewish history and are still blown in Israel today.

When the service was over Mahesh came to me and said, "You look so familiar."

"I'm Sheila Walsh," I said. "I interviewed you a couple of years ago when I was cohost of the *700 Club*."

Mahesh began to weep, and he called his wife over. "We prayed for you when you were in the hospital," he said. It was a sweet reunion.

After the meeting we went back home. Eleanor has since gone back to her doctor and learned that her cancer cell count is half what it was. It was 800 before, now 405. It could be a remission or a gradual healing. Before the service her cancer cell count had been doubling every time she went for a checkup.

Sometimes God answers our prayers for healing. Other times He seems so silent.

WHEN HEAVEN SEEMS SILENT

No subject in this book tears at my soul more than what I want to share with you now. Across the land and around the world, thousands of believers pray fervently for healing or for relief from terrible pain or other difficulties. Every week when I was cohosting the *700 Club*, calls from people in heartbreaking situations flooded the phone lines. And as I have traveled with the Women of Faith Conferences I've spoken to even more people:

- The fifteen-year-old girl, living rough on the streets of Chicago, who asked, "Can God be interested in someone like me?"

- The eight-year-old boy who wrote, "You say that God can do all sorts of things. Please ask God if He'll make my mommy love my daddy."

- The young man who told me he had been a homosexual for the past twelve years. When he told the elders of his church that he had given his life to the Lord and wanted to make everything right, they told him, "There is no place for homosexuals in our church."

- The young girl who called me, saying she was being sexually abused by her father and her uncle. She couldn't turn to anyone for help because no one would believe her.

The list can go on and on. There are innumerable situations where you want to see God's hand move and make a difference, make everything all right. Yet heaven often seems silent, mute, uncaring.

Why?

I don't know the answer. I don't believe that anyone fully does. But God has brought some very brave and godly people into my life who have helped me to understand that there are no easy answers and to accept living with mystery when there is no visible reason to do so.

Debbie, a dear friend of mine, is a victim of the most debilitating form of multiple sclerosis. The first time I talked with Debbie was when she called the *700 Club* in the late summer of 1989 and asked for me. She told me a little bit about herself, how she had been a regular on her college volleyball team—the picture of health—and then one day the pain from MS started.

She told me she watched the *700 Club* every day, sometimes three times a day at different hours. But she admitted we were a mixed blessing: "I'm twenty-five, I'm dying of MS, and I'm scared. I love God, and I know ultimately I'm going to be in heaven—that's not the question. But I'm really scared, and you of all people should be the ones to help me. Why do you seem to be afraid to talk about the fact of death?"

I didn't have an answer for Debbie that day. I told her I would pray for her and that we would talk again—soon.

Debbie's call haunted me. The more I thought about it, the more I realized that we could easily come across as if we were saying, "How dare you not get well? We've prayed for you. It can't possibly be our fault because we pray very good prayers. If you haven't gotten well, there must be something in your life, some kind of sin, that keeps you from being healed."

WE'RE ALL ONE HAPPY BAND, UNTIL . . .

As the dog days of August 1989 passed, I looked forward to the special Labor Day services for everyone involved with CBN and Regent University. There are no broadcasts, and we all get together to fast and pray. Nevertheless, I couldn't get Debbie's agony out of my mind. She was dying by millimeters each day, and our broadcasts seemed at times to be pouring acid in her wounds in the name of the Lord.

Toward the end of our Labor Day time together, Pat Robertson got up to give his annual message on what he believed God had ahead for the *700 Club*. Before he spoke he said, "If you have something on your heart you feel God has given you, I want you to come up and share it now."

I stood up and began to talk about Debbie—how much she loved the *700 Club*, yet how she also had such real doubts and fears. Then I said:

"As I was praying about Debbie just yesterday, a picture came to my mind—a very clear impression of how we as a church march along like a very triumphant, happy little band, and any time members of our band fall down, we pick them up, dust them off, and give them a quick prayer. If they recuperate, they continue marching along. If they don't, they fall behind, but we don't even know. We never look back to see if they made it or not. If they come with us, fine, but if they don't, it's their problem.

"And what does the Lord think of all this? I can imagine Him saying: 'This must never happen. I'm tired of coming along behind you to pick people out of the gutter when that's really your job. It's time that you carried them, because that's what the Christian walk is all about. If I choose to heal them, I will. If not, I want them to go from your arms to Mine; don't drop them by the wayside.'"

All across the room there was an awful hush, and I could hear one or two people sobbing. "Thank you, Sheila," Pat said quietly. "That was a good word." And then he led a prayer for all the people who were hurting, for those who were bewildered, for those who were waiting for God to answer their prayers.

I know our Labor Day experience together made us all more sensitive to those who face long-term or terminal illness. After that we did several specific shows on death and dying.

When I Saw Debbie, I Was Shocked

But that's not the end of Debbie's story. Not long after we met on the phone, her mother wrote to me: "If you want to do anything for Debbie, now's the time because we only have a few more months at the most. Is there any way I could bring her in for a weekend to meet you in person and talk with you?"

I called, and we made arrangements to have Debbie come, accompanied by her mother. When I saw her in the studio audience of the *700 Club* that day, I could not conceal my shock. Debbie was thin, pale, with dark circles surrounding her eyes. She looked so fragile, as if a puff of wind would carry her away.

As we became acquainted, I could see that for Debbie everything was a tremendous effort, even breathing. She is fed through a tube that has to be replaced every three weeks, and she told me of the terrible discomfort involved every time the tube has to be put down her throat into her stomach. Her doctor is a very compassionate man, and each time he starts to insert the tube, he tells her, "You know I love you, Debbie."

One time, while trying to change the tube quickly, with as little pain for her as possible, he got it jammed and it started choking her. He tried to yank it back out, but it would not move. While still conscious, she could hear him calling for a gurney to get her to the operating room.

They rushed her down the hall. She was still conscious and thinking, *I'm dying. I've only a couple of minutes . . . I know I'm dying.* Once in the operating room, there was no time to give her an anesthetic. The doctor simply took a scalpel, opened her stomach, and pulled out the tube. Then to numb the pain, he gave her a massive dose of something similar to morphine.

Debbie survived that incident, but every three weeks she knows it could happen again.

I asked her, "In the midst of something like that, where is God? In the midst of the panic, where is He?"

Debbie shared honestly with me about her fears and her

disappointment in having so few Christian friends or church members who were willing to talk with her about her plight.

"Surely the church should be the one group of people who could help me die," she told me. "But they're the people who don't want to talk about it because they feel it's a lack of faith. I think it's because they're afraid. Why should I be afraid of heaven? Heaven is supposed to be such a great place, why should I be afraid? I ask them, 'Why won't you walk that way with me?'"

At one point I said to her, "Do you ever wish you'd just die?"

She nodded her assent and explained, "Three times I've prayed, 'Please take me now.' But then out of the corner of my eye I would see my mother, hanging in there, willing me to make it, and I would make myself make it for her sake."

SHE NEVER FEELS ABANDONED

Debbie and her mother came to see me twice while I was still at the *700 Club*, and we talked often on the phone as well. They have both become my good friends. Debbie, always thinking of others, asked me, "Will you be there for my mom when I'm gone? Will you be there for my mom?"

We've talked about the funeral, what should be done and how. Through it all, Debbie is very honest, very real, and full of incredible faith.

Once when Debbie and I talked on the phone in 1990, she told me of how her condition continues to deteriorate. She has such trouble breathing that oxygen has been installed by her bed so she can take it when she feels she needs it. But she's had a couple of frightening incidents when she had the oxygen up as high as it would go and she still didn't seem to be able to breathe.

"I couldn't even tell it was on," she said. "My pulse was weak, and my mom was standing there. I could see terror in her eyes. She wanted to call for an ambulance, but I didn't want to die in a hospital. I knew this was it. I knew I was going, and I wanted to die at home. But when I saw how scared my mother was, I realized I couldn't put her through this."

Debbie was taken to the hospital that night, and the doctors were able to stabilize her condition. But she lives from day to day, her bones so weak and fragile that she can dislocate her hip if she brushes against something. Her left arm is in a cast because she broke it simply by bumping against a wall.

I asked her if she felt abandoned during the moments when she thought, "This is it!"

She said, "I know for sure that if I did die, it would be okay. I've never felt abandoned. In fact, the funny thing is that I feel closer to Jesus at these times, but I'm still scared. There are still so many scary elements. I look at the anguish in my mother's eyes, and I know how she wants to hold on to me one more day. But over and above all that, there is a peace, and I know that if this is the moment that I'm going to die, it will be okay."

DEBBIE ASKS THE SEARCHING QUESTIONS

I treasure the letters Debbie has written to me because they state so beautifully the hopes, fears, and incredible faith of someone who is dying slowly and in great pain but who trusts God anyway. In one of her letters, Debbie asked the questions that puzzle all of us:

> Does God hear my prayers?
> Why are some people healed while others are not?
> Is my faith strong enough?
> Why did it seem at first that I was all alone?

In that letter Debbie answered these questions from the perspective of someone who has every reason to give in to despair—but doesn't.

She said: "Through all of my illness, I have had so many questions and thoughts going through my mind. I've tried very hard to find some answers and, although I will never know all the answers, I have come to be more comfortable with some of the very many struggles that being terminally ill brings."

"DOES GOD HEAR MY PRAYERS?"

"I used to ask myself," she continued, "if God knows I will lose anyway, why does He make me try so hard to win? In struggling with this issue I've come to the conclusion that there are times when, regardless of the score, just to be alive is to be winning.

"I used to think that maybe my faith wasn't strong enough. As you know, when I got down on my knees to pray I got the dislocated hip. I guess that's what I get for being bound and determined. When I pray it comes right from the heart, and I do appreciate and thank God for *every* day.

"I'll take the good and the bad. I want to live. You would think that I'd get used to all this frustration, severe pain, drastic change of life, and the long, lonely times I have to sit in bed thinking of what it's all about while I have tubes and bottles and needles connected to my body. I don't think you ever get used to it; at least I don't, but I do know while all this is happening I keep my personal relationship with Jesus Christ a very honest, open relationship.

"I know that at the times when I have not been able to walk, talk, move, even breathe on my own, God has carried me."

"WHY ARE SOME PEOPLE HEALED AND OTHERS NOT?"

"My life has kind of been like walking through the snow—every step shows. I wonder how many people feel the way I do about not being healed. I know that I am not alone, and I want to be an example to people to let them know that it's worth holding on. Yes, it does get hard and, yes, it's an up-and-down situation. But overall, life is worth living.

"If I knew that I've helped even one person—then I would be happy and feel like I've done what I've set out to do. Sometimes I wonder if God isn't giving me this time to reach out to others in similar situations. I feel as if there is something I still have to accomplish before I die. I pray I can. I want others to know they must accept Jesus into their lives so they can have eternal life.

"As I always say, only those prepared to die are really prepared to live, and as one of my favorite songs says, 'It is well with my soul.'

"I'd like people to say they are *living* with their diseases, not dying from their diseases. We have to know that being terminally ill is not a punishment from God."

"IS MY FAITH STRONG ENOUGH?"

"Since I was told that I do have a disease and that I am going to die, I have had a new way of looking at life. I realize how fragile life really is. At first I took a quick look at the Lord and a long look at my problems. I've learned to change this around, and now *I take a quick look at my problems and a long look at the Lord.*"

"WHY DID IT SEEM AT FIRST THAT I WAS ALL ALONE?"

"My illness has taught me many lessons, some very painful. Being terminally ill brings many changes in our lives, lifestyles, families, and friends. My family has never left me. They have always stuck by my side, always pulling for me, and for this I am ever so blessed. Most of my so-called friends have not stuck around and have decided to let me go through this whole, long, painful ordeal alone with my family. I guess most can't face the fact that I am going to die, but I wish they would realize that someday they are going to die, too, and that I'm still the same old me, maybe just a lot more fragile and thinner, but I still think the way I always have.

"I got sick at a time in my life when I was just beginning to live. I had a lot of expectations: to be married, to have kids of my own, to be able to pursue a career, to be able to take care of myself, to raise my own kids the same good way I have been raised, to be able to give back some of the joy I have received in my life.

"I think a lot of my expectations have been crushed. I will never be called Mom by my own children. My mom and dad and sisters take care of me, including dressing me, helping me with medicine, IVs, injections, tubes, oxygen, feeding machines. Again, for this help I am very blessed.

"I've also learned that you should never take things for granted. Life is too short and fragile. I used to be very afraid of going to sleep at night because I was afraid I wouldn't wake up. I can't tell you the many, many nights I've lain in bed, thinking so many thoughts and saying so many prayers. Lately, I've decided to start saying, 'If I should wake up before I die.' It helps."

Debbie later shared how many have sat by her bed and, like Job's comforters, told her there must be some secret sin in her life. (I wonder if they feel her lack of healing reflects badly on their prayer lives?) This "comfort" has left her to bear her pain alone. But in the midst of this spiritual maelstrom, Debbie still trusts Jesus.

———

Turning Point: When God seems far away and our prayers bounce off the ceiling, we can give in to despair, or we can keep holding on to heaven in simple trust.

———

I, on the other hand, have struggled with Debbie's pain. I can accept her inevitable death. I believe that "to be absent from the body . . . [is] to be present with the Lord" (2 Cor. 5:8 NKJV), so death is something we can all look forward to. We are waiting for death to bring us face-to-face with God. But I struggle to accept the suffering Debbie must endure before her death.

Debbie called me one night over a year after we had met. The pain was more than she could bear, and she needed to talk.

After a long conversation, I hung up the phone, angry with God. "If You're not going to heal her," I cried out, "then take her home. Why, why must she suffer so much now?"

I opened my Bible and read Romans 8:36–37:

> "For Your sake we are killed all day long;
> We are accounted as sheep for the slaughter."
> Yet in all these things we are more than conquerors
>   through Him who loves us (NKJV).

Debbie isn't being a conqueror, I thought. *It seems as if she is being conquered daily.*

I stayed up all night struggling to make sense of this horror. I would love to tell you I found the answer to my question about why Debbie must suffer. But I didn't. I did find, however, a key to being conquerors: faith and the love of God.

Paul wrote to the Romans about the sufferings he and his companions endured. Their flesh was tormented, sometimes daily, but they were conquerors because they believed in God and trusted His love through Christ. "Neither death nor life, nor angels nor principalities nor powers, nor things present nor things to come, nor height nor depth, nor any other created thing, shall be able to separate us from the love of God which is in Christ Jesus our Lord" (Rom. 8:38–39 NKJV). Knowing nothing would keep God from loving them, Paul and his companions were able to keep believing in God and loving Him by walking with Him and proclaiming the gospel.

Conquerors are satisfied to know God loves them. Pain

and death may destroy their bodies. But they know their souls will live forever because of the love of God. Thus, conquerors can live with unanswered questions, as Debbie does. They don't confine God to a box of neatly packaged answers. They are able to depend on God without demanding explanations as if God "owed" them something.

Although she has not been healed, pain and death have not destroyed God's love for Debbie nor has Debbie's love for Jesus been destroyed. Debbie believes in God's love, so she can remain faithful until she is with God in heaven.

Our comfort is knowing that God is for us and nothing can keep us from His love. Our God is powerful. His love overcomes the powers of life and death and makes us more than conquerors.

Relatively few of us face, or will ever face, the pain and suffering Debbie and her family have experienced. Most of us, however, can relate to how it feels when all of heaven seems to be silent and we see no solution to a hopeless situation. Many biblical personalities knew that feeling, particularly our good friend Job.

Don't Let Suffering Embitter You

Surely Job understood the feeling of abandonment that comes when the silence of heaven is deafening. He told his friend Eliphaz he could feel the arrows of an all-powerful God poisoning his being (Job 6:4). Like Debbie, he wished for death, but death did not come.

So anxious was Job for an audience with God that Job was willing to take his life in his hands and go before his Maker to plead his case rather than continue to listen to his friends smear him with their lies (13:3–4). At one point Job said, "Though he slay me, yet will I trust him" (13:15 NKJV).

Always, Job's real intent was to trust God *no matter what happened.* But as his suffering went on, day after painful day, he was driven to complain:

> I cry out to you, God, but you do not answer;
> I stand up, but you just look at me.
> You have turned on me without mercy;
> With your powerful hand you attacked me.
> You snatched me up and threw me into the wind and
> tossed me about in the storm.
> I know you will bring me down to death (30:20–23 NCV).

Frustrated by God's silence and the continued attacks of the men who had come to be his "comforters," Job showed that he was very human, just like the rest of us. He couldn't understand why his prayers seemed to bounce off the ceiling. It seemed to him that God was attacking him without mercy. He wanted to trust God, but it all seemed so unfair.

It was at this point that Elihu came on the scene, and in his lengthy speech he gave Job a warning we all need to hear: "Watch out! Don't let your anger at others lead you into scoffing at God! Don't let your suffering embitter you at the only one who can deliver you" (Job 36:18 TLB).

That's the answer I heard Debbie giving me in her letter. *God is the only One Who can deliver us, and we must trust Him.*

No matter what happens, no matter how inexplicable life can be, we must trust God rather than give in to despair. I thank the Lord daily that in Women of Faith Conferences I meet people who model this kind of trust in amazing ways. I believe in miracles and have seen and talked with people who have experienced miracles. But the truth is, and Jesus demonstrated it again and again, miracles are not the real point. Jesus didn't do miracles for everyone. He didn't heal everyone. He performed healing miracles in certain situations to glorify God and to build the faith of those He touched. But always He wanted people to understand it is faith that honors God, whether miracles occur or not.

When pain and despair clamp down with jaws of iron, we wonder whether such faith is possible. Yet I've seen Christians trust God when everyone else, even the healers and evangelists, have given up.

RANDY HAD BEEN EVERYBODY'S GUINEA PIG

I met Randy, a young man in his early twenties, while singing in a missions convention in Hawaii. One of his legs was badly twisted from an accident he had had as a child. The main speaker at one of the evening meetings was to be a well-known Christian leader who had a reputation for extraordinary healing miracles. I was to sing first, and then he would speak. All day before the meeting, I kept thinking of Randy, who worked with a missions organization in the Hawaiian Islands. He loved God with a radiant faith and never questioned Him.

Wouldn't it be wonderful, I thought, *if Randy were healed—if tonight he ran right out of that meeting with his leg made whole?*

That night I finished singing and left the platform and sat down with high anticipation. During his message, the guest speaker said, "I want everyone in this place tonight who is not well to know it is God's will to heal every single person."

I could hardly contain myself. I was sure I was going to see an incredible miracle that would strengthen my faith as nothing else had ever done. The speaker assured us that he wasn't special and that he had no healing power. In fact, God could use any of us if we were willing, and then he offered an invitation to anyone who wanted to be able to pray for people so they could be healed to come forward.

Eagerly I went to the front, and around two hundred other people joined me.

After the speaker prayed for us, he said, "If anybody is sick, I want you to come up and let one of these people pray for you."

A young girl came up to me and said she had a sore tooth, and I thought to myself, *Okay, God knows that I had better start with a sore tooth.* So I prayed for her, all the time trying to see over her head to where Randy was sitting. After I prayed, the girl said her tooth was better, and I thought, *That's great—that is really wonderful . . .*

After much praying for those who had various ailments, there was a great deal of rejoicing and commotion as many said that they, indeed, were healed. Then the speaker moved on, the evening came to a close, and the speaker was whisked out a side door and was gone.

As the room emptied, I went about gathering up the tapes I had used for accompaniment while I sang. As I turned I saw Randy, sitting in a corner with his leg as twisted as ever.

I wondered what to do. Should I just slip out, or should I go over and talk to him? What would I say? But I couldn't worry about that. Everybody had left him, and he was alone. I knew I couldn't leave him too.

I sat down beside Randy and put my arm around him, and we just sat there for a long time, not speaking. After probably ten minutes Randy finally said: "You know, Sheila, you feel a lot worse than I do right now."

"What do you mean?" I said, not believing my ears.

"Well, I'm used to this. I've been everybody's guinea pig. I've had everybody who wants to be Kathryn Kuhlman pray for me. I've gone to healing meetings. I know God can heal me, and for a few moments tonight I thought maybe . . . but my faith is not based on my healing. My faith is in Jesus."

Randy's words reminded me of what David Biebel wrote in his penetrating book *If God Is So Good, Why Do I Hurt So Bad?*: "Pain has two faces, human and divine. The human face is haggard, drawn, contorted and streaked with tears. The divine face is calm, assuring, kind and loving, but likewise, streaked with tears."[1]

When I left Randy that night I had very mixed feelings. I felt a tremendous sense of injustice and yet I also realized that Randy had been the strongest one in the room. And he had drawn his strength from only one thing: His faith was in Jesus, not in miracles, and he knew God was faithful even when He seemed far away.

WHY ARE WE AFRAID TO BE
HONEST WITH GOD?

I've shared the stories of Debbie and Randy to make one point: For all of us, there will be times when God seems far away and prayers bounce off the ceiling. It is at these moments—whether we face terminal illness or are being terminated at work—that we must choose. We can give in to despair, or we can keep going on in simple trust.

As I said in Chapter 2, however, I believe that we can trust and still ask questions. To question God is not to lack faith, although some Christians say that. When someone close to them is hurting, they seem to feel the need to contain that person's pain. They want to gift wrap it because the force of that pain might make them question their own faith.

Questioning God sounds blasphemous to some people. They might say, "How dare you? Who do you think you are, that you can come before God and question Him?" But I don't think being honest with God is blasphemous at all. I believe God wants us to be honest because He wants a real relationship with us, not something plastic or halfhearted.

I sometimes ask myself how it must feel to be God and love people with a passion so great that You would give Your only Son to hang on a cross and be ripped in two. How must it feel to know that that kind of love is the very essence of Your being, and yet day after day You can see that Your children are hurting, but they only come before You simply to say, "Well, thank You, Jesus, for another day"? They never open up. They are never honest. How that must grieve God's heart!

David Biebel made an apt observation when he said: "Why are hurting people sometimes asked, expected or required to pretend about the way they really feel when telling the truth is closer to godliness than pretending will ever be?"[2]

I believe God much prefers to have His children come before Him and say, "God, this makes no sense to me. I hurt so badly. I just don't understand. I don't think I'll ever understand, but, God, I love and trust You, and I rest in the fact that You know how I feel. You've been there. You've had Your heart ripped out. I can't understand what is happening to me, but help me to glorify You through it all."

I want to end this chapter with the story of Marolyn Ford, a woman who kept on trusting God even though her prayers seemed to bounce off the ceiling year after year. Marolyn is one of those people who patiently wait for God's answer to come. Her story has the same happy ending as Job's, who was twice as well off after he withstood Satan's attacks and chose to accept whatever God gave him.

SHE WAS BLIND AND NOW SHE SEES

When she was eighteen, Marolyn Ford's sight began to fail. Soon she lost all of her central vision and could no longer read, write, recognize people, or drive a car. All that remained was a little peripheral vision that made her aware of light and good-sized objects nearby.

She was examined at the Mayo Clinic, and the diagnosis was macular degeneration, which had ruined the retina in both eyes. Doctors were sorry, but nothing could be done. She would be blind for life.

A committed Christian since the age of nine, Marolyn had started praying for a godly husband at the age of twelve. She knew God wanted to use her in ministry of some kind, and she was sure she was supposed to marry a minister.

Marolyn went on to college, but not to a school for the blind. She completed her studies and earned her degree by listening to tape recordings of lectures, taking oral exams, and spending untold extra hours to pass all of her courses with excellent grades.

While in college she met the man who would become her husband. They married and had a daughter. By then, even the tiny bit of peripheral vision had vanished, and she was totally in the dark.

Throughout her entire ordeal, Marolyn kept her inner eyes on Jesus, realizing that she would have to go on with her life. She said, "If you're going through the valley, through the tribulation, accept it as from the Lord. I didn't have to like my blindness, but I needed to learn to accept it. I knew the Lord had a reason for it, and my prayer was, 'Dear God, if I have to be blind, let it not be in vain.'"

While Marolyn was willing to accept whatever happened, she often asked God to give back her eyesight. Each time she and her husband prayed, they were reminded of the apostle Paul. He had an affliction—some say it was his eyesight—and he prayed that the Lord would take that affliction from him. But each time he prayed it seemed that the Lord would say, "My grace is sufficient for you." And each time Marolyn and her husband prayed, it seemed as if the Lord were saying, "No, Marolyn, I have a reason for you to be blind."

"I CAN SEE! I CAN SEE!"

Marolyn and her husband knew the Lord could heal. They continued to trust, believe, and hang on. One night after coming home from church, where Marolyn was the choir director, they got down on their knees to pray once again. Her husband cried out to God, asking Him for healing of Marolyn's eyes. Suddenly, inexplicably, miraculously, Marolyn could see perfectly. She shouted, "I can see! I can see!"

Her husband said incredulously, "What do you mean, you can see? You mean you can make out some dim objects or something?"

"No, I can see your face. I can see you. I can see everything!" For the first time she could look into the face of the man she had married. For the first time she could see her darling little girl.

It was a total and wonderful miracle. Three days later, Marolyn went to see her eye specialist. She walked into the office as any sighted person would do and easily read his eye chart. Then he spent a great deal of time peering into her eyes with all of his various instruments.

Finally, he stepped back and said, "Marolyn, you walked in here and read the letters on my eye chart, and it's obvious you can see, but medically speaking your eyes are still blind. When I look into your eyes, all I see is black scar tissue where it should be smooth and pink. There is no medical explanation for why you can see with those two eyes."

At first, Marolyn was disappointed because she had thought that God had "healed her completely." But then she realized that the return of her sight was an even greater miracle. She has shared her story with thousands of people throughout the world, strengthening the faith of many Christians and bringing many other people into the kingdom. It has been almost ten years since the miracle, and she still thanks God every day that her blind eyes now see.

Marolyn Ford's testimony gave a real lift to my own faith. I believe with all my heart that God can do miracles, but I have never before seen a miracle like Marolyn's. I pray for more faith to believe what God can do, but I also thank the Lord that so many other Christians have been models of faith and commitment, even though they have not been healed.

Whenever God seems to be silent, we face a critical turning point. We can give in to doubt, frustration, anger, depression and, finally, despair because it is all too much to bear. Or we can hold on to faith, just as Jesus did when He faced Gethsemane, the mockery of a trial, floggings, crucifixion, and, worst of all, the moment when God turned His face from His Son.

Rebecca Manley Pippert was my guest on *Heart to Heart* in 1990, and she shared many helpful insights from her new book *Hope Has Its Reasons*. I recommend that you obtain a copy, because it contains excellent counsel on what to do when God seems to be silent. Becky's words say it so well for Debbie, Randy, Marolyn—and all of us:

"Jesus' resurrection scars also prepare us for the fact that there may be pain in our lives, too. There may come a time when little makes sense and when evil and chaos seem to be winning the day. There may be times when we feel hopelessness and confusion, when we do not see even a flicker of light and the lesson of Jesus' scars is to hold on, to be patient and to trust God, even when we cannot see any reason to do so."[3]

Life is tough but God is faithful.

9

A CIRCLE OF FRIENDS

═══

When we feel weak and overcome, we can wallow in self-pity, or we can choose to reach out and help one another.

*B*ack in the fall of 1990 I sat anxiously by the phone, waiting for news from my friend. The ring shook the air and sent me jumping out of my chair. I picked up the receiver.

"How did it go?" I asked.

One of my best friends had recently joined Alcoholics Anonymous after struggling for a long time on his own and getting nowhere. I was glad he was finally getting some help. But I was nervous. Would they understand him? Would he feel accepted?

"Sheila," he answered, "for the first time in my life, I realize what the church could be."

"What do you mean?"

"Well, I stood up, told them my name, told them I had a problem, and they understood and accepted me. The room was filled with people who knew they couldn't make it on their own. We needed each other."

I was happy my friend had begun the long journey home. But I was also intrigued by his comments. God's Word teaches us that when we are weak, then we are strong. So we should be most free to admit our needs in church. But instead, so often we feel obliged to grin like Cheshire cats so we will be "good witnesses."

—————

Turning Point: When we feel weak and overcome, we can wallow in self-pity, or we can choose to reach out and help one another.

—————

The world is not looking for Stepford-type Christians. People are tired of pretense. We struggle with failures; we long for intimacy. So why are we feigning perfection before God and one another?

Perhaps it is because we misread passages like James 5:16: "Confess your trespasses to one another, and pray for one another, that you may be healed. The effective, fervent prayer of a righteous man avails much" (NKJV). We think *righteous man* means "superhero." So we search for the ultra religious person who can save the day—or attempt to be that person ourselves.

When we do this, we miss the truth that confessing our trespasses and praying for one another makes us the righteous men and women who can bring about healing from God. We become righteous by admitting our weaknesses to one another, and we gain healing and strength through others' prayers. When we try to become superheroes, we become more deeply entrenched in our failures rather than find healing.

HIDING OUR PAIN AND LONELINESS

In 1990, when I was cohosting the *700 Club,* I was surprised by an onslaught of letters from believing women who claimed their husbands abused them:

> "Sheila, my husband is an elder in our church, but he
> beats me. Please help me."
> "I know that I have to submit to my husband, but he
> makes me feel so worthless. What can I do?"
> "My husband is so determined to control me. I feel as if I
> am disappearing. I feel alone."

I had just rejected material for a program on men who abuse women, thinking the topic irrelevant for our audience. After receiving all the letters, I invited Dr. Margaret Rinck to be a guest on my show and to respond to this issue.

Dr. Rinck told me that this little-talked-about issue was a much greater problem than the church wanted to admit. Women feared going forward for help, thinking they would not be believed or feeling they should suffer in order to "lay up treasure in heaven." Men refused to admit their behavior, believing they needed to maintain the appearance of perfection and control.

The picture was distressing. Men and women were suffering daily. People needed healing and support. Yet everyone was hiding the truth, because of the mistaken idea that Christians don't have such problems.

Like James, John proclaimed the freedom and healing that would come from confession of sin. "If we walk in the light as He is in the light, we have fellowship with one another, and the blood of Jesus Christ His Son cleanses us from all sin. If we say that we have no sin, we deceive ourselves, and the truth is not in us. If we confess our sins, He is faithful and just to forgive us our sins and to cleanse us from all unrighteousness" (1 John 1:7–9 NKJV).

Walking in the light means we are cleansed by the blood of Christ and able to have fellowship with other believers. We will be constantly cleansed, wrote John, if we confess our sins as they surface. When we hide our sins and cover our weaknesses, when we pretend to be Christian supermen, we live in denial—"the truth is not in us." We then become isolated from one another and from God.

I think one of the greatest cancers of our day is loneliness, the way we hide our imperfections and doubts from one another. I think it's time to tell the truth.

My son, Christian, loves cupcakes. I frost them with a dark chocolate frosting. One day I was going out and had on a white cotton blouse and jeans. He saw me come into the kitchen, and he yelled "Mom!" and threw his arms around my neck and rubbed his grubby little face in my hair.

I thought, *This is how God invites us to come to Him. Not to clean ourselves up, but to come and bury our face in the mane of the Lion of Judah. Come as we really are.* It wouldn't cross Christian's mind to clean up before he hugged me because I have on a white blouse.

When I talk about the love of God to women in Women

of Faith Conferences, that's what I talk about. That passage in Isaiah 61:1 says:

> The Spirit of the Lord God is upon Me,
> Because the Lord has anointed Me
> To preach good tidings to the poor;
> He has sent Me to heal the brokenhearted,
> To proclaim liberty to the captives,
> And the opening of the prison to those who are bound
> (NKJV).

So many women in the church live in a dark place because they are so ashamed of themselves and so full of questions and have no place to bring that pain. I want to encourage people to bring their doubts and their questions and the broken pieces of their life to one another.

Can you imagine what freedom would come to the body of Christ if we could stand up and say, "Hello, I'm Sheila, and I'm a sinner. I need your help to make it."

In 1992 I began to receive counseling to help me deal with my father's death. For too long I had filled the ache with noise and service. But I was ready to take off the bandages and allow fresh air and sunlight to touch my wounds. I was ready to admit I needed help. I was ready to lay down my pride and acknowledge I couldn't heal my own pain. It was hard to be exposed as flawed and imperfect, but an airtight bandage will prevent a wound from healing.

When I was in the hospital later that year, group therapy, which is somewhat like an AA group, was very healing for me. I could talk out my doubts, questions, and fears with the other people there. However, one person in our group (I'll call her Mary) sat there every morning and said nothing. There were only eight of us. Still she said nothing.

She was about fifty, and fit my childhood vision of a typical missionary. Short, straight hair, no makeup, sweater up to her neck—and she just sat there. I kept wishing that she would tell us anything about her life.

One morning somebody said something (I don't remember what; it wasn't all that significant to me), and suddenly this woman got up, picked up her chair, and threw it against the wall! Then she laid on the floor and wept.

Once Mary stopped crying, we discovered the reason she was there. When she was twelve, her sister's husband had raped her, and she felt it was her fault. She became a missionary to make up to God for the fact that she had been a "bad girl." All those years she had hated the mission field. But she stayed there because she had this tremendous guilt that she must have done something to make her brother-in-law do this. She thought she had to spend the rest of her life paying for it.

It was as if we were discovering this whole other person. We all got down on the floor and put our arms around Mary and said to her, "You were just a little girl." "It wasn't your fault."

Another person in our group was a pastor of a large church. He had become so severely depressed that he had tried to take his life. He said, "The reason I am depressed is that I don't know if anything I believe is true anymore. I have spent my whole ministry telling people to do things I can't do myself. Telling them to live up to things I am not living up to myself." He felt his whole life was meaningless.

I thought of the book *Telling the Truth: The Gospel As Tragedy, Comedy, and Fairy Tale* by Frederick Buechner. It has a wonderful story about how the role of the pastor—or anyone—is to stand in the pulpit and simply tell the truth.

If you don't tell the truth, everyone in the building knows you're lying. You are the loneliest person there.

I discovered that in my own life. I spent so many years in ministry trying to be inspirational, trying to show what it would look like if someone sold out to God. Now I know that my apparent perfection left a gulf between me and other people. My open brokenness was the first bridge that allowed people to cross over and come to me.

It's hard to admit helplessness over our behavior and to ask for help. But I don't want to live in the chains of pride and fear. I want to find healing and to share life with other believers. Admitting our need for help to quit being victims or abusers or addicts or hypocrites can free us and the generations to come. I want to live with real people. And I want to be real too.

Perhaps some of us walk with a limp. Perhaps we will always have scars. The One we follow has carried His scars for a long time, and He longs for us to show Him ours so He can heal them.

And He longs for us to reach out to one another as servants and fellow travelers on this treacherous journey called life.

A SERVANT AND FRIEND

I only knew a little of trying to be a servant when I was younger. Now I can see that every church should offer a course on Footwashing for Beginners. From the moment we come into the kingdom of God, we need to be helped to understand a basic principle laid down by Jesus Himself: "Whoever wants to become great among you must serve the rest of you like a servant" (Matt. 20:26 NCV).

So many passages of Scripture are familiar to us, and yet I wonder how much time we take to meditate on the implications of these words for our lives on a daily basis. Sometimes, for example, I like to imagine what the scene must have been like the evening of the Last Supper when Jesus gave His greatest lesson on servanthood.

Before sitting down to a meal together, it was Jewish practice to be sure that everyone's feet had been washed. Open sandals were standard footwear, and all the roads of Palestine were dry and dusty. By the way, animals—whose masters were seldom concerned about where their animals left their waste—shared those same roads. To maintain Jewish standards of cleanliness, it was necessary that everyone's feet be washed before sitting down to eat a meal.

In most Jewish homes, a servant would be at the door with a pitcher and a towel, ready to get down on his or her knees to wash the feet of guests as they arrived. But on the night of the Last Supper, there was no servant. There were only Jesus and His twelve followers.

Picture the scene: The first disciple arrived, looked into the room, and saw that no one was there doing any foot-washing. *Typical*, he said to himself. *They haven't gotten anyone to handle it. Well, I'm certainly not going to do it.*

And so that disciple reclined at the table, his feet unwashed. Then two more disciples arrived and, seeing one disciple already at the table, thought to themselves, *Well, if he's not going to do it, I don't see why we should do it.*

And so they reclined also, followed by the rest of the

disciples, until they were all gathered around the table—twelve grown men with dirty feet!

When Jesus arrived, He, of course, didn't have thoughts of *Well, this certainly isn't for Me; after all, I'm their leader.* Instead, Jesus saw the opportunity to teach His disciples one of their most important lessons.

The meal was barely underway when Jesus, the King of kings and Lord of lords, knowing what lay ahead—the spiritual, emotional, and physical turmoil that would tear His soul apart—stood up and took off his outer clothing. John, in his Gospel, described what happened next:

> Taking a towel, he wrapped it around his waist. Then he poured water into a bowl and began to wash the followers' feet, drying them with the towel that was wrapped around him (John 13:4–5 NCV).

He got all the way to Peter before there was any protest. "Oh, no, no, no, Lord!" Peter objected. "You don't need to do this. No, please sit down. One of us should have been doing it in the first place."

But by then it was too late, because Jesus had looked right into their hearts and could see them as they really were—and as we all are.

Jesus knew what it meant to be a servant. I wish we all could follow in His footsteps. Unfortunately that doesn't always happen.

When I first met Debbie, the young woman with MS, she shared how many people have sat by her bed and, like Job's "comforters," told her there must be some secret sin in her life. But in the midst of this spiritual maelstrom, Debbie still trusts Jesus.

When I saw her in 1997 she told me, "My illness hasn't affected my faith in Christ the slightest, but it has affected my faith in other believers. So many of the people who originally prayed for me and visited me have found the journey too long. They have stopped coming. It would have been a relief for them if I had died sooner. I've lived too long for what they have to give me."

She told me that she would welcome death. She said to me, "My pastor doesn't come see me anymore; would you conduct my funeral service?"

I told her I would probably have to do it in conjunction with a pastor, but I agreed. She wants me to sing "Peace Like a River."

Thankfully I've finally learned how to be a friend to Debbie and other women.

WOMEN OF FAITH

The Women of Faith Conferences are something I've always searched for but wouldn't have been ready for until now. If I had gone on the road with these five other women earlier in my life, I would have tried to impress them—to prove I deserved to be on the team.

Just after I got out of the hospital, I returned to California. George Otis, a friend of mine, asked if I would sing at one of his High Adventure Ministries Seminars.

"George, I'm not doing anything in public," I said. "I really feel that I need some time away from the spotlight. I need to heal and to continue to learn what God is trying to teach me."

"Sheila, this is a conference, specifically for those who are ministering in countries where they would lose their lives if their presence was known. There will be no publicity. No one will know you are going to be there. All I want you to do is come and sing one song."

"Okay," I said, "but the only reason I am coming is because I love you and would love to see you."

I decided to go for the whole conference, rather than just for my part. It was a small conference, maybe forty people. I sat and listened to those incredible men and women who put their lives on the line to communicate the gospel. That day they told us what Christ was doing in Muslim nations, things they couldn't share publicly.

I sang "How Great Thou Art." Two weeks later I got a two-page letter from one of the couples. The wife wrote, "As you were ministering to us through song, the Lord gave me the following words of encouragement for you."

The letter talked about me having a son—yet I wasn't even married at the time. It said, "Your son has a special protection over him. The Lord will guard his heart as you guard your own heart. 'I'll provide for him,' says the Lord. 'I will protect and guard him. Just continue loving him, for he wants to make sure that you still love him. As long as he has that assurance, he'll be fine.'" (Later, when I was pregnant with Christian and the doctors thought there might be something wrong with him, I kept pulling their letter out of my Bible to read it.)

The letter listed three things God was going to do for me. "The Lord will give you a new song . . . The period of boot camp is over, and it is time for promotion." And then she said, "I will bring new women into your life. You will be an instrument of love in their ears. There will be opportunities to minister to women globally."

Before I had been in the hospital, I didn't even relate well to women. My best friends were always men; I felt safer with guys because they didn't talk so much about real stuff.

One prophecy was absolutely on the button. (God is so kind to do that—to give us a glimpse into the future.) "A new book has opened in your life . . . a new way of life and a new thinking. A new heart and new eyes. Suddenly you will begin to see life differently, you will see yourself as a new person."

Once I got out of the hospital I was ready to take my eyes off myself. Now I could really see other people. I was similar to the blind man Jesus healed. The Lord washed this man's eyes, and he said, "I see men like trees, walking" (Mark 8:24 NKJV). So Jesus washed that man's eyes again and he could see people as they really were.

I spent the first thirty-five years of my life seeing people as trees. Now I see people differently and am prepared to allow them to really see me.

The organizers of the Women of Faith Conferences asked me to start speaking when Christian was only six weeks old (I had intended to wait until he was four months old) because one of the speakers couldn't go to Hawaii. Barry and I and our baby went. We had everything with us, since I didn't know what I'd need—a Portacrib, car seat, play mat, toys, and books.

I sat on stage with all the other women. (It's so great that the format calls for us all to be there together rather than to come in to speak individually and to leave right after. Talk about a circle of friends!) One after another the ladies stood up—Barbara Johnson, Patsy Clairmont, Lucy Swindoll, Marilyn Meberg, and Thelma Wells. They all seemed to be whistling the same tune. These women had been through devastating things—yet in the midst of all their difficulties, they had known how to really laugh.

I wanted to stand up and say, "Yes, this is true. This will get you all the way home—not just two or three miles down the road."

I cried all through that conference. I finally felt that God said, "You are home." I had found companionship with a circle of friends.

A pastor's wife came up to me after one Women of Faith Conference and said, "I want to thank you with all my heart for giving me permission to be human."

We get hundreds of letters saying something like this: "This was the first time I could be myself. I know now I can be real. And I can reach out to other people."

After one of our conferences in Florida, I was back at the hotel with Christian. Two women came up to me. They looked to be in their sixties and seemed so alike they could be sisters. They both hugged me and then told me how the conference had impacted their lives. Eight years ago one of them had found out that her son was living a gay lifestyle and is HIV positive. The first thing she had done after my session was to tell her sister about her son. For eight years she had carried this sorrow alone. Now her sister could help her.

Jesus knew that we need to offer each other understanding and grace.

GRACE AND THE BIG BIRD

I was on tour with my British band in the fall of 1983. We had given sixty-three concerts in three months, and I was suffering from bus fever. A pastor in a small Kansas town had asked if we could come and do a concert for him after our Kansas City date. He told us that no one ever came to his little town, so we said yes.

The night before the concert we arrived in this tiny town, exhausted. We pulled up to our motel and looked it over skeptically, unsure of what we were in for. It far exceeded any of our expectations—even with shoes on, we stuck to the carpet!

We were more prepared for the concert the next evening. The pastor had told us there would be only about fifty people at the show, but they would be very appreciative. And just as he said, at concert time, fifty people came through the doors of the church. For some reason unknown to me, forty-nine of the people sat in the back three rows of the church, and in the front row one man in a bright yellow T-shirt sat alone.

As I opened with the first song, I felt as if all the fruit of the Spirit had fallen off my tree. We sang our songs, and the forty-nine people in the back clapped politely. But "Big Bird" in the front never clapped once. I began to get annoyed. *Why does he have to sit in the front row if he's not going to clap?* I wondered. I decided that he had come to annoy me and that it was working. I began staring at him after songs trying to shame him into clapping, but he wouldn't respond.

When the concert was finally over, I sat in the pastor's study, bemused and self-pitying. Suddenly someone kicked

139

the door. I opened it, and there stood my adversary in yellow! He was smiling from ear to ear. "You will never know how much tonight has meant to me," he said. "I have all your albums, and I've asked God for a long time to bring you here." As I looked at this gracious, loving man, I realized that he had no arms.

I don't think I have ever been so ashamed in my whole life. In my need for approval, I had judged someone who had faithfully prayed for me for years. I had judged him based only on what I could see.

As I lay in my freezing cold waterbed at the motel that night, I asked God to forgive me. And then I asked myself some questions. "What if the man had had arms and was genuinely there to annoy me? Would that have given me an excuse for rejecting him?" Not if I was going to respond with grace. Grace is unmerited favor; grace gives mercy and love when we don't deserve it.

The Hebrew word for *grace* means "to bend, or stoop." Donald Barnhouse, the late pastor and Bible scholar, painted a beautiful picture of grace when he said, "Love that goes upward is worship, love that goes outward is affection, love that stoops is grace." When we didn't deserve it, God stooped down by becoming a Man to love us. I needed to stoop down from my place on the stage, from my needs, to love the man in my audience.

One of the best books I've ever read is *The Grace Awakening* by Chuck Swindoll. I wish that it were mandatory reading for every believer. It is a book of life, of freedom, of the overwhelming grace of God.

Chuck came on *Heart to Heart* to discuss the book and told a story similar to mine. While he was speaking at a conference, he was distracted by a man who kept falling asleep during his sessions. Finally, after the last session, the man's wife approached Chuck. He straightened his back and placed his hands on his hips, preparing himself to accept the woman's apology for her husband's behavior.

Instead of offering an apology, however, the woman reached out and shook Chuck's hand warmly and thanked him for his messages. Her husband was dying of cancer, she told Chuck. His medication made him drowsy at times, but he wouldn't miss Chuck's sessions for the world. The woman continued talking as Chuck's shoulders slowly sank.

It is easy to judge quickly when we see only what is before our eyes. But when we look at others with the grace Christ has shown us, we can see beyond the outer shell to the human heart. As Paul said in 2 Corinthians 5:16, "we regard no one according to the flesh" (NKJV) because of the grace of Christ in reconciling us to God. Now we can have the patience to try to understand what is happening inside others and love them so they can be reconciled to God too.

Our churches and our witness to the world would be transformed if we could extend this mercy and love to ourselves and then to each other.

A TRUE CIRCLE OF FRIENDS

One Sunday before Christmas of 1998, our pastor stood up and said, "We are going to have a child baptism this morning."

I was surprised, as we had been waiting for the next baptism service so Christian could be baptized, and it wasn't scheduled for three more weeks. I knew one of the couples in our church in Nashville was expecting a baby. The father sang solos sometimes. I had heard that they had a little girl, Hope, who was born with a rare degenerative illness. Only about six people in America have it.

The disease comes from a recessive gene, and both parents have to have this gene for a child to be born like that. The young couple had no clue that anything was wrong until the baby was born.

The pastor told us, "Hope is being baptized today because we don't know if she will live through Christmas." He didn't try to make this okay; instead he said none of us understand this.

The whole congregation stood, and their small group came up front to stand around the couple. The whole church was in tears.

"We know that the minute Hope closes her eyes down here, she will open her eyes with the Lord," the pastor said. "This mom and dad named their child Hope before they knew what was wrong."

Surely this is a picture of the church in the new millennium. We stand with one another. All weeping. No one there that day had a sense that we could make it okay for this young couple. How could we insult them by suggesting that anything could make it okay? But we could say, "We will be with you in offering this child up to the Lord."

That's a true circle of friends.

10

IS HEAVEN REALLY SILENT?

When life is tough, we can give up, or we can come before the Lord with our problem—and wait patiently for His answer.

Cathy Mahone was swept off her feet by Ali Bayon. A dark, handsome man from Jordan, Ali had come to college in America, where he met Cathy. Although he was a Muslim, religion was never an issue between them. Cathy had little interest in spiritual things, and Ali didn't practice his faith.

A year after Cathy and Ali were married, Cathy became a Christian. Ali was content to let her read the Bible and attend church as long as she didn't expect him to accompany her. Cathy prayed God would one day change Ali's heart. She didn't expect the change that did take place.

When Cathy was five months pregnant, Ali visited his family in Jordan by himself. He returned a different man. Now fervently committed to Islam, Ali began to insist that their child be raised in the Muslim faith. Dumbfounded,

Cathy did her best to keep peace in the household until Lauren was born. Then she and Ali argued constantly. A year later, they divorced.

Cathy and Ali managed to establish a fairly amicable relationship, with Ali frequently seeing his daughter.

When Lauren was seven years old, Ali took her for the weekend, promising to drop her off at school on Monday morning. Monday afternoon, Cathy arrived at school to pick up Lauren. But she discovered Lauren had never been there.

Kidnapped! Cathy panicked. She knew instinctively what had happened. She ran inside the school and called the airport to confirm her suspicions. The airport personnel told her that Ali and Lauren had, in fact, left for Jordan that morning.

Cathy immediately called the State Department, but they could offer little help. According to Jordanian law, the father has all legal rights to a child when the child is seven years old. So Ali had the right to take Lauren as his. The State Department promised to try to help Cathy but informed her that she was only one of many such cases.

Unable to bear going home to an empty house, Cathy checked into a cheap motel. She fasted and prayed for three days, begging God to speak to her. She opened her Bible and began to read in the book of Daniel: "Do not fear, Daniel, for from the first day that you set your heart to understand, and to humble yourself before your God, your words were heard; and I have come because of your words" (10:12 NKJV).

Daniel had prayed for help for twenty-one days and heard no answer. When the angel finally appeared to him, he told Daniel that God had heard Daniel from the first day he prayed. "But the prince of the kingdom of Persia withstood me twenty-one days; and behold, Michael, one of the chief princes, came to help me, for I had been left alone there with the kings of Persia" (Daniel 10:13). The angel had immediately been sent to help Daniel but was held back by a strong spiritual power of darkness. Because Daniel kept praying, the angel received more help and was able to come to him.

Daniel's story gave Cathy hope to keep on praying. She knew she had done all she could do physically. Only God could bring Lauren back. Cathy left the hotel and went home, committing to pray each day and to wait.

Prayer is definitely one of the turning points in our walk with God. When life is tough, we can give up or we can come before the Lord with our problem—and wait patiently for his answer.

JOB WAITED

Bildad, the Shuhite, was the first person to mention prayer in the long discourse between Job and his friends. Bildad began his statement to Job by saying, "If you were pure and good, he [God] would hear your prayer, and answer you, and bless you with a happy home" (Job 8:6 TLB).

Later, after Zophar added his recriminations to the other two friends' accusations, Job threw up his hands and said, "Look . . . I understand what you are saying . . . Oh, how I long to speak directly to the Almighty. I want to talk this over with God himself" (13:1–3).

As I read that, I wondered, *Didn't Job pray?* And then as I thought further, I realized that probably he did. Yet, like us, he needed a special communication from God to keep going, a special sign or fleece.

Job continued, saying he was going to argue his case with God. Job's points of defense were:

- I know I am righteous.

- I am frail, as are all men. (How can You demand purity in one born impure, as You created us?)

Throughout this time Job's anger was increasing, but he was not burying it within himself. He was allowing God to hear his disappointment. I believe that's what God wants for us. He isn't angered by our honest expression of unhappiness. He's able to take the heat!

At the end of the Women of Faith Conferences in Chicago, I stood at my table for maybe two hours talking with women. One woman stood to the side. (Often that means the person would like a private moment and is willing to wait until that is possible.) I had someone keep an eye on her to make sure that she remained where she was. If she had begun to leave, I would have broken away and taken a moment for her right then.

By the time the line was over and Barry was putting the covers on our tables, the woman came over to me and threw her arms around my neck. She said, "I want to congratulate you on your son. You love that little boy."

By this time Christian was about a year and a half old, so I was surprised by her enthusiasm. Still I said, "I really appreciate that."

"Let me explain to you why that means so much to me to be able to do that."

We sat down together at the table, and she told me that

she had lost two children. The first time she was devastated but the doctors, her husband, and the church said it wouldn't happen again. "We will see you through it, and everything will be fine," they assured her. "Your child is safe with the Lord."

The next pregnancy was a repetition of the first. She went nine months and delivered a dead baby. The second time she began to hate God and to hate any mother who had a child who would be the age of hers.

"I listened tonight when you spoke of forgiveness," she said, "and it is the first time it has made sense to me. I realized it was okay for me to beat my fists against God's chest and tell Him, 'I don't understand and I'm angry.'

"I finally forgave God and forgave myself for feeling all the bitterness. I wanted you to be the first woman I congratulated on her child."

That woman had learned a lot about our heavenly Father through her devastating experiences. She now knew He would listen to her anger. Job came to the same realization.

About halfway through the back-and-forth struggle between Job and his friends, Job cried out, "Oh, that I knew where to find God—that I could go to his throne and talk with him there. I would tell him all about my side of this argument, and listen to his reply, and understand what he wants. Would he merely overpower me with his greatness? No, he would listen with sympathy" (Job 23:3–6 TLB).

Even in the middle of his anguish, Job knew that God is faithful and would listen to him. Still Job was wanting a direct confirmation from God. A special sign.

Some, like Job, look for such a special communication from God. Others, like Ruth Graham, have found worship in prayer as an answer to their distress.

WORSHIP AND WORRY CANNOT
EXIST TOGETHER

I have very few heroes. I'm not cynical about people, but I am fairly realistic. We believers are merely frail human beings, doing our best with the grace of God to be more like Jesus. I do have one or two heroes, though—my mother being one and Ruth Bell Graham another.

You don't get to see very much of the elegant, gifted lady who has stood behind Billy Graham for years. Ruth once said if she became too recognizable she would dye her hair and move to Europe! At crusades she prefers to sit among the crowds of people—not on the platform—as her beloved husband brings the only message of hope for a hurting world.

Ruth is gifted in her use of words and has a wonderful sense of humor. A talk show host once asked her if in all her years of marriage she had ever considered divorce. "Divorce—never; murder—often!" she quipped. Ruth is one of my favorite poets; she often expresses my exact feelings through her carefully penned words.

If I were allowed one word to describe Ruth Bell Graham, I would choose *faithful*. There must have been days when it was difficult to be the wife of such a well-known man, times when it would have been good to have him home to help in a family crisis or to share a special sunset.

In 1991 I spent some time with Ruth in the Grahams' lovely mountain home in North Carolina. Mementos of years of faithful service to Christ across the globe and in her home surround her there. Pictures of her children, grand-children, and great-grandchildren adorn every tabletop.

She's the mother of five, grandmother of nineteen, and great-grandmother of three.

I asked Ruth how she handled the tough days as a young wife and mother. How did she respond when she was, at times, pushed into an unsolicited spotlight? Her answer was simple yet profound.

"Worship and worry cannot exist at the same time in the same heart," she said. "They are mutually exclusive."

Ruth then told me about a time when she awoke in the middle of the night, concerned about one of her children. Unable to sleep, she got out of bed, picked up her Bible, and began to read: "Be anxious for nothing, but in everything by prayer and supplication, with thanksgiving, let your requests be made known to God" (Phil. 4:6 NKJV).

Ruth realized that the missing ingredient in her heart at that time was thanksgiving, so she began to thank God for this son, for his life, for the joy he had brought to their home. Her burden lifted, and she fell back asleep.

———

Turning Point: When life is tough, we can give up, or we can come before the Lord with our problem—and wait patiently for His answer.

———

We can pray and make our requests known to God, but we have to trust that God will answer our prayers. Thanksgiving helps us do that. When we pray with thanksgiving, we are saying we believe He will answer us and provide for our needs or for the needs of those we love—and we will be happy with His provision.

Offering thanks helps us release control, acknowledge God's strength, and rejoice that He can take care of what we have brought before Him. It frees us from our worries and allows us to rest.

I am thankful for that night with Ruth Graham. We continued to talk after she told me her story until it was time to turn in for the night. Ruth made me some hot tea, which I took to my room. After I had crawled into bed, a little picture on the wall caught my eye. It said, "Edge your days with prayer; they are less likely to unravel." I knew that was how this faithful woman lived.

She knew God answered her prayers. And God answered Job's continuing prayers.

From Out of a Whirlwind

Job got his wish. God joined their theological discussion in a dramatic way, speaking from a whirlwind.

He asked Job to remember who God is and who Job is. God's answer to Job's questions began with the oft-quoted phrase: "Where were you when I laid the foundations of the earth? Tell me, if you know so much" (Job 38:4 TLB).

Then God reminded Job of all that God controls—and what little Job knew or understood. He challenged Job, "Do you still want to argue with the Almighty? Or will you yield? Do you—God's critic—have the answers?" (Job 40:2 TLB)

And finally Job gave control of his life to God, just as I did one Sunday while I was in the hospital. In the middle of that week I had asked if I could have a pass to go to church. The doctors said I could and a nurse would accompany me.

I didn't know any churches in the Washington, D.C., area, and when I asked the nurse about this she said, "I've gone to a small Episcopal church near here. What about going there?" That sounded okay to me.

That Sunday was one of those beautiful Indian summer days; even though it was fall, the sun was shining through the church's stained-glass windows. I sat at the back and listened to those old traditional hymns washing over me. It was so healing.

The pastor said, "Some of you in here feel as if you are dead inside. Christ is here in all His resurrection power. If you will simply call on Him, He will reach into that place and pull you out."

I had given my life to Christ in my bedroom and so had never walked to an altar in my life. Yet I quickly asked the nurse if I could go forward; she said it was fine. I ran to the front of that church and lay flat on my face in front of the altar.

It was the first time I had gone to God empty-handed. Before I'd always gone with a new book or a new record or a new something I'd done to make God love me.

Nothing in my hands I bring; simply to Thy cross I cling, I thought that day. I'd never felt so ashamed. I felt like I came as a filthy, broken, bedraggled orphan. "There's not a thing in the world I can do to make You love me," I said to God, "but I also realize there's not a thing in the world I can do to stop You from loving me." It was the first time I offered nothing to make Him love me. Yet I felt such peace.

Christ reached down and gathered me to His heart. I finally gave up.

It's one of those great paradoxes of faith—it stops you in your tracks, yet it sets you free. You give up control and you feel so free. I get it clearly now—it has nothing to do with me.

Now when they introduce me to speak to thousands of women at a Women of Faith Conference and I'm exhausted because Christian is cutting a tooth and I have had no sleep, I don't have any of the old panic. Every night before I go up on stage I say one word, "*Yes. Yes* to everything, Lord, and *yes* to being Your instrument."

Finally, Job also gave up control of his life. He admitted, "I am nothing—how could I ever find the answers? I lay my hand upon my mouth in silence. I have said too much already" (Job 40:4–5 TLB).

Yes, Job! You got it!

Job went on to say, "I know that you can do anything and that no one can stop you. You ask who it is who has so foolishly denied your providence. It is I. I was talking about things I knew nothing about and did not understand, things far too wonderful for me" (42:2–3).

God answered Job's prayers, just as He does ours, and then He called Job's friends to accountability.

FORGIVE THOSE WHO HAVE WRONGED US

After God admonished Job's three friends—Eliphaz, Bildad, and Zophar—He told them, "Take seven young bulls and seven rams and go to my servant Job and offer a burnt offering for yourselves; and my servant Job will pray for you, and I will accept his prayer on your behalf" (42:8).

Told by God to do so, these friends finally repented. And

then Job prayed for them, forgiving them for all the wrong they had done to him.

That surely wasn't easy for him. Forgiveness is tough, just as life is tough. It's very hard for many of us to forgive those who have wronged us in some way. I have had to forgive, and yet I always struggle with it.

My earliest memory of this is still a vivid one. My mother had recently painted the banister in our home and had banned sliding down it. But it was so tempting! The banister was long enough so I could pick up speed as I slid down and then be launched into space at the other end. I fought with the flesh and lost. I positioned myself at the top of the stairs with my new sandals on and slid down. As I looked back, I realized with horror that the buckle of my sandals had scraped all the way down, leaving a trench in the new paint. At that moment my brother, Stephen, appeared and said he was going to tell my mom. I begged him not to. (Didn't I realize that she would probably notice it?) He told me that if I gave him my large bag of candy, which I had been saving for a showing of *Cinderella* on TV that afternoon, he would remain closemouthed.

I looked at the candy. I looked at the long scratch all the way down the railing. It was a painful decision, but I traded my bag of candy for his silence.

Stephen sat on the bottom stair and ate every piece. Then he went and told my mum! I was devastated—and also had a very sore sit-upon after Mum spanked me! I was overwhelmed by the injustice of the situation, especially when my mother told me that it was my own fault.

A few years later I was faced with a more serious situation. A friend lied about me to my two closest friends, and I could not defend myself without betraying the trust of someone dear to me. I spent many sleepless nights and wept many bitter tears, feeling helpless and betrayed. But in the midst of it all, I was faced with Christ's command to forgive so that my heavenly Father would forgive me.

I read Jesus' words on forgiveness in the Sermon on the Mount one afternoon. Jesus had been teaching the disciples to pray simply and in secret—not like the hypocrites who prayed on the street corners, vainly repeating themselves. The model for the prayer He gave them included forgiving others and asking for God's forgiveness: "Our Father in heaven . . . forgive us our debts, as we forgive our debtors" (Matt. 6:9–12 NKJV).

At the close of the prayer, Jesus emphasized this, saying, "For if you forgive men their trespasses, your heavenly Father will also forgive you. But if you do not forgive men their trespasses, neither will your Father forgive your trespasses" (vv. 14–15).

God will have no mercy on us if we recognize someone else's guilt and refuse to forgive him. "Judge not, that you be not judged," Jesus said later in His Sermon. Don't spend time trying to remove a speck from someone else's eye when you have a plank in your own. Remember your own need, Jesus was saying. When we refuse to forgive, we are setting ourselves up as a judge and demanding that others be perfect—something we can't do. God will judge and demand perfection of us when we judge others.

When we forgive, we see through other people's behavior to their need. We recognize their guilt and at the same time see our own. We realize that we won't find justice in this world—it doesn't live here. So we give up the fruitless, heartbreaking search for it, and we give mercy to those who have wounded us.

I know of some who have limped into eternity with rope burns from the millstone of unforgiveness deep in their ankles. How do we cut the cord? In my case, I asked God to bless the girl who had wronged me. I asked Him to pull her close to His heart, believing that she had to be pretty miserable herself to lie about someone. I remembered my own need and was finally able to choose to forgive.

At times when I saw her my anger would stir up again, so I would once again lift her up to the throne of grace and ask God to bless her. Only in remembering my own need for forgiveness could I choose to forgive. I didn't feel like forgiving. I chose to forgive, and then I felt like it.

But the person I needed to forgive the most was my father. When I was in the hospital, the doctors asked me if I had ever written a letter to him. I thought, *That's stupid. My father's dead.* And that's what I told the doctors.

"You're doing this for yourself," they said. "We recommend you write it with your left hand. If you write it with that hand, you are less confident and not so in control. You will write what you really think and feel."

I waited until I got out of the hospital. Then I sat down and wrote with my left hand. I was surprised at what poured out. I was angry at my dad for leaving me, for not being there when I was a child and when I was married, for me feeling responsible for my mother as a child. As if it were my fault! All those years I spent trying to be the perfect daughter so I wouldn't add any more pain to my mother's life.

I felt a peace at forgiving my dad for being human. It wasn't his choice to walk away from me; in fact, those same experiences had been taken away from him. And I forgave myself for excluding him from my life because I couldn't deal with my memories.

I flew home to Scotland and asked my mom if she knew where my dad was buried; I knew she had not put up a gravestone because she had no money. She remembered and we drove there and she left me alone. I read my dad the letter. The cemetery was quiet, and I felt a companionship with my father I had never known until then. Finally I forgave my father for what he had no control of—and I forgave myself.

Others have walked this way before. Another woman waited after a Women of Faith session until the people had gone so we could be alone. She said, "I'm seventy years old, and tonight I have forgiven my brother."

About fifty-five years ago her brother had raped her. She had carried the baby to term and then given the infant up for adoption. "For fifty-five years I've hated my brother and hated myself. Tonight I finally forgave him. I am going to call him and tell him so."

What happened to Job after he forgave his friends?

Scripture tells us that the Lord restored his wealth and happiness. In fact, the Lord gave him everything back—twice blessed.

Where he formerly had 7,000 sheep, he now had 14,000. Before he had owned 3,000 camels; now he had 6,000. Formerly he had had 500 teams of oxen; now he had 1,000. Formerly he had had 500 female donkeys; now he had 1,000. And God gave him 7 more sons and 3 more daughters.

God expects us to forgive. That's why he made confession and forgiveness a part of the Lord's Prayer, indicating its place in every prayer time.

Does God hear our prayers today as He did in Job's day?

Yes, and many stories in this book prove that. As does the ending to Cathy's experience.

HELP CAME AFTER PRAYER AND FASTING

Cathy didn't have to wait long for the first help to come. Only a few days later, one of a four-man covert commando team of former Delta Force fighters heard of Cathy's plight and contacted her. He brought the team to meet with Cathy, and they planned to fly to Jordan and bring Lauren home. Three of the men were Christians and felt that God had sent them to fight on her behalf. The men told Cathy they would probably be executed if they were caught. But they were committed to the mission.

The men left for Jordan, promising to call Cathy when their rescue was complete. The code of victory was "The sun is shining."

For the next month, Cathy waited by the phone with no word. She finally decided to fly to Jordan to join the men.

The first day after Cathy joined the team, they spotted Ali's car on a side street. The rescue mission was underway.

Phase One: The group would follow Lauren's school bus the next morning and hold it up in the countryside. Phase Two: They would make a dash for Israel. They would be safe once they crossed the border.

Damp fog shrouded the city the next morning. Cathy's heart pounded as she and the men got in the car and followed Lauren's school bus, maintaining a careful distance from the bus. As soon as the bus left the city limits, the rescue team sped up, overtaking the bus and making it stop.

Cathy leapt from her car, raced into the bus, and grabbed a startled Lauren.

Packed into the car, Cathy, Lauren, and the team headed toward the border. The fog slowed them, and Cathy wondered what would happen when they were pulled over at the checkpoint. She held Lauren tightly to her chest and looked out the car window. A few miles away, she saw the Israeli border. And through a break in the clouds, the sun was shining. Cathy knew they were home free.

Today Cathy and Lauren are together. Lauren prays every night that Jesus will touch her father's heart. Cathy has learned not to be discouraged by the apparent silence of heaven but instead to keep praying. Wars as real as those on earth are waged in the heavenly realm on behalf of those who love God.

11

GOD HAS LEFT US
A JOB TO DO

===

When the needy cross our path, we can choose to
show selfish indifference, or we can take our eyes off
our own needs and follow Jesus to love the unlovely.

*I*t was hot and sticky. The air was filled with dust
as we landed in Manila in January 1988 to film
a TV documentary about the work of Compassion International, a Christian child sponsorship agency. I
had worked with Compassion for almost six years. From
Los Angeles to New York, I would often speak in my concerts about the difference Compassion makes in the lives of
the children who are born with so little.

I knew all the statistics. Three out of every five children
are born in Third World nations, and *one in three of those*
will die before they are five years old due to the ravages of
malnutrition and disease. While we spend millions on the
latest diet craze, children die for lack of a piece of bread.

Compassion had invited me to help bring the enormity of the problem to the attention of people back in the United States. I was more than willing to be involved in helping God's people understand our opportunity to reach out to those whose silent screams break the Father's heart.

As we left the air terminal, an incredible scene assaulted our senses. I've never seen so many people in one place at one time—all moving, all pushing, all going in different directions. I was falling over children and chickens at the same time, trying not to scratch the several mosquito bites I had suffered in the past three minutes. The Philippine gentleman who came to pick us up grinned from ear to ear.

"I think it will take us some time to get out of here, yes?"

I agreed, but I didn't care because I was having too much fun. As I stood on the roof of a truck to take photos of the heaving masses, I felt like Indiana "Walsh" in *Raiders of the Lost "Airport."*

Our friends in the film crew had already arrived and were hard at work. We spent the first couple of days visiting various Compassion projects—schools, villages, wells, and water pumps.

On the third morning we made an early start because the school we were due to film was some distance away. I got up at 5:00 A.M. to shower, and as I did my makeup for the cameras, I thought, *This is all a bit pointless. In this heat I'm just going to melt, drip, and run anyway.*

By 7:00 A.M. we were all in the Jeep and heading out across the dusty roads. We arrived a little before 9:00 and wandered in to watch the classes in progress. The little school had begun with one teacher and two or three children, but through the prayers and hard work of the local people and the support of Compassion, it had grown significantly.

Each time the school grew too big for the building, they simply added another room. It was no architectural masterpiece, but it spoke of those who have a dream and never give up hope.

I sat with the class during its morning worship service and was amazed as each child recited a memory verse. Those children knew more of the Bible by heart in their eight short years than I had learned in thirty. Unexpectedly, the teacher announced that I was going to sing "Jesus Loves Me." As I sang the well-known words, they took on a meaning I could never have imagined before going to the Philippines.

When I came to the phrase "Little ones to Him belong, they are weak, but He is strong," I knew that I was looking right into the faces of some of those little ones God cared about so very much. I felt overwhelmed by a sense of God's compassion for each one.

BELINDA WAS ONE OF TEN CHILDREN

One girl in particular caught my eye. She seemed shy, very quiet, very small. I asked the teacher about her and learned that her name was Belinda and that she had no sponsor, so I said I would love to be her sponsor.

As school broke up for the day and the children scattered outside, screaming and yelling, much like children anywhere, someone suggested that we might go and meet Belinda's family. We took a Jeep as far as we could and then set off on foot, deeper and deeper into a kind of shantytown. The homes were built over a swamp, and the stench from the open sewers was almost unbearable.

Our Philippine interpreter went on ahead to explain to Belinda's mother who we were and why we were there, but I felt uncomfortable. How would this poor woman, who lived in a one-room shack with ten children, react to our uninvited invasion? A cameraman was with us, and I wondered, *Had we come to meet this woman or just to pump up our TV special?*

Nothing could have prepared me for the love that poured from that woman's heart toward me. She threw her arms around my neck and wept on my shoulder. I began weeping too, and we clung together, total strangers, surrounded by her ten children crawling through the mud and chasing skinny chickens out of the room that was their kitchen, living room, and bedroom all in one. I glanced over to the corner. A cockroach was crawling over the baby, and I wondered whether this little one would make it.

As we stood in the doorway, the mother told me through an interpreter the things that brought her joy and the things that broke her heart. I looked at her eight daughters, and I wondered what the future held for them. What kind of wedding would they have? What would they wear? Where would they live?

I looked into the woman's eyes and was surprised by her hope and courage. She said, "The Lord's presence fills my home, and His glory is with us." We prayed together as best we could with our mixed languages, and I turned to leave. As I walked away, tears blurred my vision, and I stepped off the plank right into the mud. I stopped to wipe the tears from my eyes, and when I looked down, there was Belinda's mother, on her knees in the mud, trying to wipe off my shoes as her children looked on with concern.

I couldn't speak. I could only give Belinda and her mom one more hug, and then I hurried away.

As we worked our way back to the Jeep, a member of the film crew asked, "Are you all right, Sheila?"

"Yeah, I'll be okay if you just leave me alone for a few moments."

I wandered off across the field, my only companion a lethargic water buffalo. Manila was still hot, sticky, and dirty, but I would never be the same.

A SONG WAS BORN IN THAT SWAMP

A few days later, as the wheels of our jetliner left the tarmac of Manila's airport, words from Jesus' well-known parable kept running through my mind: *I was hungry, and you gave me food. I was thirsty, and you gave me something to drink . . . anything you did for even the least of these my people here, you also did for me* (Matt. 25:35—40 NCV).

Already I was thinking about a song that would someday appear on one of my albums. When I got back to the States, I teamed with Rod Trott and Jon Sweet to do "Angels with Dirty Faces," which eventually became part of the album *Say So*. I admit that the lyrics take poetic license of sorts, but there is still an important message there. Scripture tells us that when we reach out to strangers, we might be entertaining angels without knowing it (Heb. 13:2). Who is to say? Perhaps we meet angels more often than we think. As the song puts it:

This one is black
This one is white
This one is running away
This one is you
This one is me
This one is dying to stay.

Each one with our own unwritten story
Comedy, tragedy, farce
Looking for love on the road
To glory at last.

We're all angels with dirty faces
Battered and bruised by the fall
Angels with dirty faces, that's all.[1]

All of us are battered and bruised by the Fall. But when we care enough to reach out to one another in Jesus' name, we all have a future and a hope.

OUR COMPASSION IS NEEDED EVERYWHERE

The Philippines have no corner on poverty and misery. You can find the poor, the desperate, and the unlovely on the back streets of any good-sized community in America or any other country of the world. Sometimes you can find them right on your own television screen.

In 1990 I had just finished taping a special series of *Heart to Heart* programs at a celebrity mansion in Beverly Hills, California. We had filmed eleven shows in three days, and I'd talked to an amazing assortment of inspiring people, including film stars Roy Rogers, Dale Evans, Rhonda Fleming, and Pat Boone. I had also interviewed Stormie Omartian, the beautiful singer/songwriter, and Al Kasha, the Academy Award–winning composer.

My final taping had included two programs with Mario Murillo, who wrote *Critical Mass: A Strategy for a North American Revival*. *Critical mass* is a nuclear term that refers to the minimum amount of radioactive material that can and will sustain a nuclear chain reaction. Mario believes that God is looking for another kind of critical mass—a core group of Christians who will be so sold out to Him with no ulterior motives that they will bring about revival.

As Mario talked with me, he described how at times, as he prays for people, an unbearable burden comes upon him. He has to continue to pray until it lifts.

After we wrapped up the interview and Mario left, the rest of the shooting crew planned to have a celebration dinner, but I felt too tired to join them. I drove my rental car back to the hotel and sat there thinking about what Mario had said.

Never in my life had I prayed the way he had described. Never had I felt an unbearable burden where it would seem that God had shared His heart with me for a moment. I began asking the Lord if this was something He only shared with certain people who sought it and wouldn't take no for an answer.

I dialed room service, ordered a hamburger and cup of coffee, and then turned on the television set. Geraldo Rivera's show was on. I'd never seen his program, but I had heard about his reputation for being sensational.

As I reached to switch channels, I noticed that his subject

for the day was teenage prostitution. I decided to watch and see what he had to say.

His five guests were all young teenage girls who had been prostitutes on the streets of New York. They had all chosen to leave the oldest profession, and they were on the program to tell Geraldo and millions of viewers what it had been like to sell themselves on the streets.

Four of the girls were rather blasé; but one talked lucidly about not being able to live up to her family's expectations. She had been driven to living on the streets, had become hooked on drugs, and eventually went into prostitution to survive.

The girl described how unnatural her spiral downward was. No one takes the step from a fairly normal life to being a drug addict and a prostitute in one day. Instead, she took one step in this direction and another step over here, and gradually she slipped farther and farther down a chute. Before she realized it, she found herself in a situation that she never dreamed would happen.

GERALDO DID SOME "REAL LIFE" RESEARCH

As I sat fascinated, listening to the girl talk about her experiences, Geraldo broke in with a little extra surprise for his viewers. He told his television audience that as he had walked to the studio off Times Square in New York that day, he asked two young girls who were there on the streets to turn tricks to go with him to talk about who they are and why they do what they do.

The two girls were ushered onto the stage before the

cameras. They stood there, looking thin and emaciated. Geraldo pushed up their sleeves and showed their veins, wasted and bruised from drug injections. Then he asked one of the girls, "Why do you do this?"

"What else can I do?" she wanted to know. "Who is going to help me?"

The camera zoomed in on her face. I looked deep into her pain-filled eyes, and I found myself kneeling on the floor of my hotel room, weeping for those girls and for a generation of people like them who live on the streets with no hope.

Those two children were not glamorous call girls who had rolled up to the studio in their Mercedes automobiles, wearing their fur coats. Their prostitution was a matter of life and death. They didn't want to live like that, but they saw no choice.

I found myself praying for those girls, one of whom had twins just two years old. She had no idea who the father was. This wasted, sick child was the mother of two tiny lives, and she had to make enough to support them as well as herself. Half the money she made as a prostitute went to feed her children, and the other half went for drugs.

As I knelt on the floor, I felt as if God had let me see a little shadow of the pain that He feels every day as He looks across the streets of America and sees the desperation. I prayed for those two young girls and everyone they represented for a long time.

I could not forget those girls. Two nights later, I was doing a concert in Clearwater, Florida, and in the middle of the second half of my program I decided to talk about what I had seen on the *Geraldo* show. I had no idea that the emotion that had driven me to my knees two days before would come rushing back. But it did, and I couldn't go on. I don't usually cry in my concerts, but I couldn't help myself.

I paused, thinking, *Okay, I'll just take a second here and pull myself together.* But then I realized that I wasn't in control anymore, and there was nothing I could do.

I told the crowd, "I'm sorry. I know you've paid to come to a concert, but it just blows me away when I think about how God must feel about these young girls."

AND THEN GOD TOOK OVER

I got down on my knees, right on the platform, with all those people staring at me, and I began to pray. After a minute or two I looked up, because I could hear the clearing of throats and quiet blowing of noses. The whole front of the church was filled with people who had come forward to kneel or fall flat on their faces. I could hear people asking God to forgive them for their apathy and unconcern. Some were crying out to be saved.

After a while I stood up and read from Psalm 139:

Lord, you have examined me and know all about me.
You know when I sit down and when I get up.
You know my thoughts before I think them.
You know where I go and where I lie down.
You know thoroughly everything I do.
Lord, even before I say a word, you already know it.

You are all around me—in front and in back—and have
    put your hand on me.

Your knowledge is amazing to me; it is more than I can
  understand.

Where can I go to get away from your Spirit?
Where can I run from you?
If I go up to the heavens, you are there.
If I lie down in the grave, you are there.
If I rise with the sun in the east, and settle in the west
  beyond the sea, even there you would guide me.
With your right hand you would hold me (Ps. 139:1–10
  NCV).

I sang only one more song, "God Loves You." Then I
ended the evening with a prayer. But that didn't end the
evening at all. God was there, speaking to people.

A Vietnam veteran was bitter and angry because he'd
come home and found people who didn't seem to care. But
he found Jesus that night and was able to forgive.

A little eight-year-old girl said to me, "I love the Lord.
My mom's not a Christian; will you pray with me?" So I
joined hands with her and her little friend, and the three of
us prayed for her mother.

Young couples having trouble with their marriages came
forward to talk. One person after another reached out to
communicate with God—and to be honest and real, totally
open to Him.

COMPASSION IS A TWO-WAY STREET

When our plane landed at the airport before the Friday
night concert in Clearwater, I began to have despairing

thoughts about the capriciousness of scheduling. Why had I ever agreed to do a concert after spending three days doing eleven *Heart to Heart* shows and two *700 Club* broadcasts? I had gotten up at 3:30 every morning, and I was beat. Why couldn't I just go home and sleep until Monday of next year?

All day Friday I was so tired I couldn't seem to get my program for that evening organized. But I did the best I could and went over to the church for a sound check late that afternoon.

As I finished, someone from a local radio station poked his head around the corner of my dressing room and said, "I'm here for the interview that we called about."

I looked at him aghast. The last thing I felt like doing at that moment was a radio interview. But I remembered having agreed to it, so I said, "Oh, sure, come on in."

He came in, sat down, took one look at me, and said, "You know, I can see you really don't need to be doing this."

"What do you mean?" I asked as I tried to pull my professional self together.

"Well, to be honest, you really look beat. Let's not bother doing this."

"Do you really not mind?" I asked, not believing my ears.

"No, you look like you need to rest and have a cup of coffee."

He went out. He came back with a cup of coffee he had found somewhere and sat down in the dressing room. After a minute or so, I said, "Can I ask you a favor? Would you pray for me?"

"Yes, I'd be glad to pray for you," he said.

I couldn't even tell you the man's name. He was from a

local Christian radio station, in his middle to late thirties, and obviously a very kind and compassionate person. His prayer for me really touched my heart. He wasn't just somebody trying to get his job done, somebody who wanted his pound of flesh. He cared more about how I felt than about getting his interview, which is not typical of members of the media. Usually it's a case of "We don't care how tired you are; we need this for the six o'clock news."

I believe God had given this young man the gift of compassion. Whether we are gifted or not, we can all learn to be more compassionate, not only toward the poor, the downtrodden, and the unlovely, but also toward our own families, friends, and acquaintances. Again, the book of Job contains rich truth for our taking.

JOB DIDN'T RECEIVE MUCH COMPASSION

As I read the book of Job, I don't see his friends showing him a lot of compassion. Shock and dismay, yes. Willingness to spend time with him, yes. But compassion, no. Their words were laced with accusation, argument, and judgment. True, they sat with him, for seven days and seven nights in silence.

But once Job broke the silence and began to cry out in pain, his friends began a long, long harangue. Instead of comfort they brought condemnation and the accusation we still hear today: "God is punishing you for your sins."

Eliphaz, the Temanite, began the indictment. "Have you ever known a truly good and innocent person who was punished?" (Job 4:8 TLB).

To me that's an idiotic question. I wonder if Job didn't respond in the same way. I sure know plenty of good and innocent persons who have been punished by having tough times. This book is filled with their stories, people like Darrell Gilyard and Debbie, my friend who has multiple sclerosis.

Eliphaz went on. "Experience teaches that it is those who sow sin and trouble who harvest the same" (Job 4:8).

Oh, no, it doesn't. Some sinners do suffer, but lots of saints do too.

Eliphaz's advice to Job is close to what some Christians still say to their hurting friends today, "Go to God and confess your sins to him" (5:8).

Next Bildad, the Shuhite, checked in. His soliloquy is similar to Eliphaz's. And then came Zophar, the Naamathite. He began with an exhortation. "Stop," he cried. "Shouldn't someone stem this torrent of words?" He's directing his order to Job, but as a reader I think, "Yes! Someone should shut *your* mouths, not Job's."

Zophar added insult to injury. He told Job, "God is doubtlessly punishing you far less than you deserve" (11:6).

Come now, Zophar. What could be worse than what happened to Job? He'd already said he'd like to die—and that's about all the punishment that's left.

Yet these friends continued on and on. Finally Job cried out in despair. "Ten times now you have declared I am a sinner . . . you have yet to prove it" (19:1).

And he's right. Those friends spoke in generalities, but they never gave a specific instance of when Job sinned. And unfortunately that's what some of us do also.

Job confronted those friends. "Must you go on 'speaking for God' when he never once has said the things that you are putting in his mouth? Does God want your help if you are going to twist the truth for him?" (13:7–8).

We all need to heed that caution. I believe we will answer to God if we wrongly connect the suffering of our friends with their sins.

Certainly God reprimanded Job's three friends. He told Eliphaz, "I am angry with you and with your two friends, for you have not been right in what you have said about me" (Job 42:7).

Job suggested the way compassion should be expressed. In frustration, he cried out:

I have heard many things like these.
You are all painful comforters!
Will your long-winded speeches never end?
What makes you keep on arguing?
I also could speak as you do if you were in my place.
I could make great speeches against you and shake my
    head at you.
But, instead, I would encourage you, and my words would
    bring you relief (16:1–5 NCV).

Job must have felt terribly let down by his friends, who showed him no compassion to speak of. They only wanted to argue and prove him wrong, when they knew nothing of the agony that he was suffering.

When we look at Job's "miserable comforters" (and some of our own responses), we can see clearly what compassion is not. But what, then, is *compassion*? My synonym finder tells me that *compassion* is showing *pity, mercy, sympathy, kindliness,* and *concern*. But I like the way Job put it: "I would speak in such a way that it would help you" (16:5 TLB). Job was saying that if he were our friend, he would cry with us, hug us, or hold us. He would show us God's love and help us through our grieving process. Unfortunately sometimes when the needy cross our path, we choose selfish indifference.

FEAR CAN STIFLE COMPASSION

The best part of that evening in Clearwater was that I genuinely knew it was the Lord at work and not me. I am not always holy or compassionate. Sometimes I hear Jesus' call to love the unlovely, but I let those ever-present traps of fear and selfishness keep me from answering that call.

I recall a Saturday afternoon when I was in a small town where I was to give a concert in an old theater. The promoter told me not to wander too far away because we weren't in a very safe area, but I was desperate for a cup of tea. After my sound check, I looked outside the theater and realized that only a few doors down was a place where I could get some hot tea to go.

Quickly I walked to the little restaurant, ordered my tea, and was hurrying back to the theater when I saw a man coming toward me. He must have been in his early twenties, and I could tell from the way he was dressed that he lived on the streets. His hair was matted and dirty. His clothes were dirty and torn. He didn't have any shoes on his feet, and he had a strange look in his eyes.

As the wild-looking man got closer, my heart began to thump. Then he stopped me and said, "Can you give me something to drink?" I quickly thrust my hot tea into his hands and raced back to the safety and security of my dressing room. Then I forgot all about him.

That evening, the concert went well. Afterward, as I was counseling some people who had come forward to receive the Lord, I saw that same man in the crowd being counseled by some teenagers! After he wandered out, I went up to the two young people who had been talking with him and asked, "Do you know that man?"

They told me that as they were coming to the theater they had seen him on the streets and realized that he needed God's love. They stopped and asked him if he would like to come to the concert with them, and he said, "Sure, why not?" So they bought him a ticket and took him inside. Because his shirt was so torn and dirty, they also bought him a "Sheila Walsh" sweatshirt, which was on sale along with my tapes and CDs.

He put on the sweatshirt and then sat through the concert, listening intently. At the end he came forward to give his life to Jesus.

The two young people finished their story by explaining that, after leading him to the Lord, they had made arrangements to pick him up the next morning at a men's hostel, where he was staying, and take him to church.

I listened quietly as the two youngsters—a boy and a girl—shared their excitement with me. Then they disappeared into the night, rejoicing, and I was left in the strange quietness that lingers in a theater after everyone has gone home.

I sat and thought about our opposite reactions to the wild-eyed young man. I had seen him as a threat, someone who was different from me, someone who was unpredictable, possibly dangerous. The young people looked into his eyes and saw someone who needed Jesus, and they reached out to love him.

Then it struck me: That young man was like the fellow in

the Bible who had been waylaid by robbers and left bleeding by the side of the road. Life had done exactly the same to him, but I, like the priest and the Levite, had walked past to go into the comfort of the theater and present the good news of the gospel to those who already knew. The young people, however, had cared enough to be good Samaritans, to bind him up and bring him in and share the love of Christ with him.

I think it's important to remember that Jesus told the story of the good Samaritan in answer to the lawyer's question, "Who is my neighbor?" This simple story, which almost every Christian knows by heart, surely shows that we may find ourselves in situations where we need compassion, but we might not always get it. Those whom we think will offer it do not, and when compassion does appear, it comes from unlikely neighbors, indeed.

The story of the good Samaritan reminds me that the days of the Lone Ranger are over. Each one of us needs to have friends who will care for us, even when we don't deserve to be cared for. Real friendship means that even when someone falls and makes mistakes, we are still there for them. Our relationships are not up for negotiation. One of the secrets to keeping on when life is tough is to have friends who know God and love Him. Then they can reach out to know and love you as well.

———

Turning Point: When the needy cross our path, we can choose to show selfish indifference, or we can take our eyes off our own needs and follow Jesus to love the unlovely.

———

The ultimate meaning of *compassion* is *love* and *grace*. When we grasp what God's love and grace have done for us, we cannot help but show compassion to others.

HARRY WONDERED WHY HE HAD LOST EVERYTHING

One of my *Heart to Heart* guests was Harry Wingler, whose story would touch anyone. It wasn't so much his story that impressed me as the compassionate people who were guest players on his stage.

Harry had been a successful businessman with his own bakery that employed twenty-six men. He was married and had two beautiful kids, but he began drinking and experimenting with drugs, and so did his wife.

Eventually his wife left him, and the last he heard of her, she had died in the gutter as a prostitute. Local authorities moved in and took his two children away to put them in foster care.

From that moment, Harry rapidly spiraled downward. He got into financial trouble due to alcohol and drug abuse and found himself living rough on the streets. Once a well-dressed man, he now lacked a clean set of clothes to put on.

Eventually, Harry wound up living under a bridge, scraping through garbage cans, looking for some way to feed himself. He got hold of a gun, and he and a friend robbed homes. But the few dollars they made stealing were never enough. Harry's appetite for alcohol and drugs kept him penniless, homeless, and miserable.

One night he was sitting on a park bench, destitute, cold, and wet. A young Hispanic kid from a local church came up and put a tract in his hand, saying, "Tonight we have a church service. Why don't you come? God could change your life."

The kid made Harry angry. He thought, *If there really is a God, why is my life like this? Why is everything such a mess? Why have I lost everything that ever meant anything to me?*

Nonetheless, something drew him to that church. As he stood outside he could hear the music. It sounded as if they were all having a good time. It was cold outside and it looked warm in there, and so he wandered in.

He sat at the back with his gun in his pocket, watching the people singing and praising God in this small Hispanic church. The pastor looked out at him from the pulpit and told him, "God can change your life if you will let Him."

A woman who was sitting beside him fell to her knees and began to weep, crying out, "God, save my brother! Save my brother!"

"I thought she was crazy," Harry told me. "I said to myself, *I'm not her brother. I'm not Hispanic. I'm not even a close relative!*"

But Harry couldn't leave. Something about the love in that place held him fast. And before he realized it, he found himself at the front of the sanctuary, down on his knees, crying. The pastor prayed for him, and Harry, the once-proud businessman who had fallen into a rough life on the streets, gave his life to Jesus Christ and was filled with the Holy Spirit.

As he told me his story so many years after it had happened, the tears rolled down his face, as they did mine. His eyes filled with radiance and joy as he remembered the night when he stepped from darkness into light, as he remembered the radical change that God's love brought to his heart.

For me, however, this is where Harry's story really begins. The same night that he found salvation, Harry thanked his Hispanic friends and turned to leave. And they said to him, "Where are you going, Harry? You don't have a home. You're our family, now. You come and live with us."

One of the church families took him in, and he lived with them for weeks. Then the young people in the church, realizing that he didn't have anything nice to wear, chipped in with their own money to buy Harry a brand-new suit of clothes.

After a few more weeks they said, "Harry, you really need to get grounded in the Word of God." So they sent him off to Teen Challenge, where for seven months he studied the Word of God.

On that Thursday morning, with the television cameras rolling, I found myself sitting beside a man whose roots went deep into the Word of God. He reminded me of the man in Psalm 1 who was no longer walking in the counsel of the ungodly but whose roots went down deep into the river of life. As Harry left that day, I hugged him and told him what a blessing he'd been to me as well as to the viewers. Driving home later, questions filled my mind.

What would have happened had Harry come into one of our nice, white churches? Would we have loved him the way that small Hispanic community loved him? Would we have taken him home?

Would I have bought him a new suit of clothes? Or would I have gone home rejoicing that night that some homeless person had come to Jesus? Or would I have sent him "home," back under that bridge, to have his quiet time?

Finally, I wondered, *If the people in that church hadn't loved Harry and gone on loving, would he be here today with me?*

Some people might tell me, "Wait a minute, Sheila. It isn't us, it's Jesus. He is the One who draws and who keeps and who saves."

I know that, but I can't forget Harry's words: "You know, Sheila, so often we're prepared to take our hands off and say, 'Well, Jesus is the answer.'" Then he looked deep into my eyes and said something I'll never forget: "But you know, Sheila, *we* are the answer. You and me. Jesus has left us a job to do."

Harry Wingler reminded me that there is joy in doing God's will. A lovely old prayer by Ignatius of Loyola puts it this way:

> Teach us, good Lord, to serve Thee as Thou deservest;
> To give and not to count the cost;
> To fight and not to heed the wounds;
> To toil and not to seek for rest;
> To labor and not to ask for any reward;
> Save that of knowing that we do Thy will.

Saint Ignatius gave good advice. Unfortunately, we have become self-indulgent and satisfied with our westernized Christianity. We are in grave danger of staying within the comfortable confines of our own lives, failing to have compassion for others, and simply sitting at home to struggle with our own failures and temptations.

I appreciate the opportunities I've had to make missions trips to the Philippines, Poland, Russia, Bangkok, and Hong Kong. In countries like these, I've met people in desperate poverty who are still rich in Christ.

I am also grateful for needs I have been able to see in the inner city among the elderly, the homeless, those young prostitutes, and unmarried pregnant girls. We can easily find places to share a cup of cold water right in our own community, sometimes right in our own block.

I am deeply thankful to God for bringing people like Harry Wingler across my path. He is just one of many relatively unknown people who have taught me a vital secret to keeping on when life is tough. That secret is compassion. When you reach out to others in the name of Jesus, you have to take your eyes off yourself. It is then that you suddenly realize you don't have to hold on at all. Because you are so close to Jesus, He has you in the hollow of his hand.

12

THERE IS A BETTER SONG TO SING!

===

When our dreams seem to go sour or remain unful-filled, hopelessness can dominate our lives—or we can hold on with open hands, knowing that we have hope because God is faithful.

*S*ome of the most powerfully moving films are those that stir memories in our hearts. I went to see *Steel Magnolias* because I like Sally Field and Olympia Dukakis, but I sat weeping in the theater at the end because of the memories it stirred of a woman I'd known. The members of our church had watched and prayed and begged God for the life of this vibrant young wife and mother. Then we stood beside her heartbroken parents and husband and little boy and buried her.

I didn't realize when I watched *Steel Magnolias* that it was based on a true story. But two months after I'd seen it, I met the real husband. His name is Pat Robinson and his wife's name was Susan, not Shelby. Pat is a pediatrician, who, as a nine-year-old boy, was scared into the kingdom of God by a hellfire-and-brimstone message he believed into adulthood.

Pat and Susan married, knowing she had a severe form of diabetes that made it risky for her to have a baby. But Susan longed for a child, so when she conceived, she was overjoyed.

Some time after the birth of their baby, Susan became sick. Pat decided this was a test from God and he was not going to fail. He believed God was going to dramatically heal his wife as a testimony to all around her.

But Susan was not healed; in fact, she became worse. Weakened and discouraged by her sickness, she felt as if she were a failure. She believed that she had not been healed because she had no faith. So Pat decided that it would be up to him—he could save his wife.

The day Susan died, Pat was in disbelief. He stood beside her bed, and the doctors told him she was gone. But he couldn't take it in. How had he failed? How could he have been so wrong?

Pat left Susan's room and paced the halls of the hospital, wringing his hands and rubbing his forehead. Then it all became clear to him—God was going to wait until the funeral and raise Susan out of the casket! Excitement surged through him as he realized how much more impressive this miracle would be than had Susan been healed. He could barely contain himself and found it hard not to tell anyone what was going to happen.

He sat through Susan's memorial service on the edge of his pew. All around him family members wept, but he watched the casket and waited. Susan didn't sit up. The pallbearers lowered her coffin into the ground. The lid remained closed as the men threw earth over the top of it.

Pat's life crumpled like the sod on the casket. The well-meaning friends who had told him if he had enough faith Susan would be healed disappeared like the morning mist, and he was left alone with a God he didn't know.

Depression blanketed his heart as he stared into a bleak and empty future. In his loneliness he began to cry out to God. Every day he would open his Bible and read of a God who promised peace in the midst of turmoil and joy in the deepest sorrow. At first Pat's hopelessness made him feel as if he were losing his mind, and he asked God to hold on to him. As he kept his mind on God's Word and the promises that he read there, peace began to edge out his despair. He read, "You will keep him in perfect peace, / Whose mind is stayed on You" (Isa. 26:3 NKJV). He asked God to strip him of the lies and half truths Satan loves to whisper in our ears, and to reduce him to simple truth.

Perfect peace is translated from the Hebrew *shalom shalom*, which signifies *fulfillment, abundance, well-being, security*. The phrase *whose mind is stayed on You* comes from two Hebrew words: the first meaning "will, imagination"; the second, "dependent, supported, firm." When our wills and imaginations are dependent on God, when we choose to turn our thoughts to Him, we can find the simple truth that God is enough. We find out, as Isaiah wrote, that "in the LORD is everlasting strength." And in His strength we discover fulfillment and security.

Our faith in God is not enough to bring about miracles. God takes home some faithful servants before we are ready to say good-bye. And He allows people with no faith at all to be healed. All we can do in the time of grief is to set our minds on Him, to believe God is enough even if the miracles don't come, for He alone can hold us through the night.

FAITH, HOPE, AND LOVE

According to the apostle Paul, three things will continue forever: faith, hope, and love. Paul makes it clear that the greatest of these is love, and we all agree. But what of the other two?

We know faith is crucial. Without faith it is impossible to please God or to hang on when life is tough. Doubt can creep in so easily, and the only answer is to remember that Jesus is worth it all. That's the faith Pat Robinson had.

But what about hope? In our haste to be sure we have faith and love, do we sometimes fail to give hope its proper due? Without hope, life is a sorry game, played without enthusiasm or joy.

As our society marches into the twenty-first century, people wonder what our *real* chances are. Is there any *hope*?

Those are legitimate questions, and I believe that only Christians have the legitimate answers. I was reminded of this not long ago in, of all places, a movie theater.

THERE IS A PLACE TO TAKE BROKEN DREAMS

I've always loved going to the movies, and I'm the kind of person who wants to see *all* of the film. If I miss the first minute, I won't go in. I'm worse than Woody Allen. I'll wait two hours until it starts again. I like to be already seated when the lights go down so I can get into the mood of the whole thing.

And I don't like to leave until the credits have rolled. I want to know who the cameramen were, the key grip, and all the rest of the "little guys" behind the scenes who gave their all for that film.

That's why I love to go to the little arty theaters where everyone seems to feel compelled to watch all the credits at the end of the film, whether they like them or not. Most of the time in a regular cinema, people just get up and leave the minute the film is over.

In 1990 I went to see *Field of Dreams*. It's a fantasy story about a man who builds a baseball field in the middle of an Iowa cornfield, and somehow star ball players appear from the past to play on his field and give him new hope for his own life and broken dreams. The film's "theology" left a lot to be desired, but the story still had real impact on me.

As usual, when the film ended, I just sat there, trying to watch the credits while everybody kept walking past us on the way out. But as the house lights came up just a little, I couldn't help noticing the faces of the people going by. The women were smiling and chattering because they had enjoyed a good film and Kevin Costner's good looks.

But as I looked into the eyes of some of the men, I saw something else. Some of the older men, in particular, had a look of regret. For two hours they had indulged themselves in an unfamiliar luxury. They had looked back and thought about their lives, and now they were thinking, *Maybe things could have been different.*

When those men were young, they were idealistic, but now they knew that life was a matter of compromise, because that's the way life goes. You have to give and take in everything. After seeing *Field of Dreams* and thinking about how some of their own dreams had crumbled, they had looks of doubt, of wondering for just a moment, *Was I right or was I wrong in how I lived my life?*

I saw this look in the eyes of many of the men who streamed past on the way out of the theater, and it made me want to stand up and call them back in. I wanted to say: "We *can* go back. There is a place to take our disillusionment and regrets. At the foot of the cross, there is room for new beginnings."

How Rita Found Her Song

The longing look in the eyes of the men who came out of *Field of Dreams* that evening reminded me of another film I had seen years ago. *Educating Rita* is the story of a young Liverpool housewife who began to realize she could make more of her life. She enrolled in a university and began to study. A whole new world was opened for her to explore.

Soon, however, she began to feel defeated, not accepted by her family or by the academic community at the university. One night she was invited to a dinner party at her professor's home, but upon arriving at the door and glancing in the windows at all the sophisticated, formally-dressed guests, she decided she couldn't go in. Instead she went to the pub to join her husband, her parents, and the rest of her family, who were drinking beer and singing old familiar songs in typical British fashion.

Rita tried to join in with the singing, but it was all so hollow and so predictable: the men were all getting drunk, with their obedient wives at their sides, trying to look as if they were having a good time.

As the songs continued and the beer flowed, Rita looked over and saw her mother. She had stopped singing and was sitting there with tears trickling down her cheeks. Rita's mom was an average British housewife who lived by the code of just-grit-your-teeth-and-keep-going. But there she was, crying quietly while her intoxicated husband sang at the top of his lungs.

"Why are you crying, Mother?" Rita asked.

Without hesitation her mother said, "There must be a better song to sing."

Her mother's words gave Rita new hope and resolve to keep going to school. Rita's husband had taken all her books and thrown them in the fire, and she had been about to give up. He didn't want his wife to be smarter than he was. She was supposed to stay home and get pregnant, he thought.

Instead, Rita returned to the university and told her professor, "That's what I'm trying to do, isn't it? Sing a better song. Well, that's why I've come back, and that's why I'm staying. So let's start to work!"

━━━

Turning Point: When our dreams seem to go sour or remain unfulfilled, hopelessness can dominate our lives—or we can hold on with open hands, knowing that we have hope because God is faithful.

━━━

Rita had decided her better song would come by finding herself through education. She would not give up because there was, and always will be, a better song to sing.

A BETTER SONG GROWS IN BROOKLYN

On a trip to New York City I had the opportunity to attend the Brooklyn Tabernacle, pastored by Jim Cymbala, a man with a simple but profound commitment to Christ, a real man of God. I was scheduled to provide some special music for the service, which I was happy to do.

On Sunday someone from Jim's church came by to pick me up and take me across Manhattan into Brooklyn. It was a beautiful sunny day, and the church was packed. It seemed as if people of every race, creed, and color had found their way to the Brooklyn Tabernacle that particular Sunday.

The well-known Scottish poet Robert Burns once wrote, "The best laid schemes o' mice and men gang aft a-gley." That means that you can plan all you like, but it doesn't mean it's going to happen the way you've planned. How true his words are! As I always do before a concert or church service where I'm singing, I had planned to arrive in plenty of time to do a sound check in peace and quiet before the crowd came in.

What I didn't know was that at Brooklyn Tabernacle, the worshipers come in hours before anything begins. There were people everywhere. They were up on the platform where the choir was rehearsing. They were yelling up at me from the pews, asking who I was and what I was doing up there. They were coming up behind me and hugging me. I was determined that I was going to do the sound check if it killed me, and it looked as if it just might.

I guess I don't have a lot of patience some days. I just need things to go right, and when they don't I'm not thrilled. We played the first tape through the machine. It was awful.

The music sounded as if it were coming through a dirty football sock.

"I can't sing to this," I wailed. "I can't even hear it. It's terrible!"

Suddenly, it seemed as if every eye in the church was looking up at me as if to say, "Is this who is going to be singing to us? We can't bear it!"

I tried to sing through the microphone, but it sounded as if I were strangling a large cat, and I had had it. I knew I had to get out of there so, keeping my head down like a good evangelical, I headed out through the crowd of people toward the front door of the church. I made it outside, and I stood there thinking, *Lord, what am I going to do? It sounds so terrible. I don't know what to say to these people. I just wish I could run away and hide somewhere.*

GOD SPEAKS IN SPECIAL WAYS

Then I felt someone put a hand into my hand and squeeze tightly. I looked down, and there was a little girl; I suppose she was probably twelve years old. As I looked into her eyes, she grinned one of those grins that stretch from ear to ear and across the top of your head, and she said, "Isn't it great to know that Jesus loves us?"

Isn't there a saying about truth coming out of the mouths of babes? I smiled back at her and tried to say something like, "Yes, sweetheart, it certainly is." Then I turned around and headed back into the church, thinking, *Well, I guess it's time to get off your high horse again, Sheila Walsh, and join the infantry. You'll just have to march down there with all the rest of the little soldiers and take your seat at the front.*

And then I prayed, "Lord, maybe this is going to be the worst thing they've ever heard, but I give it to You, and I ask that somehow You will touch these people, because already they have reached out and touched me."

The service began. Jim Cymbala's message, which has remained with me so clearly, emphasized the way in which we bring pleasure to God's heart. It was so real and so tangible, especially his assurances that no prayer ever prayed on this planet by God's people has been lost.

"The angels hold our prayers in golden bowls up before the Father, because the fragrance of our prayers is so sweet to Him," Jim told us. "And then the angels say to Him, 'Listen, smell, see Your children praying.'"

I wonder whether you've ever prayed and felt as if your words went no higher than the ceiling. You wonder because no answer seems to appear in the mail by the next morning. Did God really hear?

That day I prayed my own feeble prayer in the front of the Brooklyn Tabernacle, saying, "O Lord, again I've been reminded of my clay feet and my fallibility. If there's anything You can do through me today, then I'm Yours, and I ask that You would wash me again and make me clean."

At that moment I knew everything would be okay. I knew and believed with all my heart that every prayer ascends to the very heart of God and brings Him pleasure.

THESE PEOPLE NEEDED A DIFFERENT SONG

As I stood up to sing, I began with one or two of my favorites from my albums. But as I sang, I looked out across the congregation and realized that so many of these people were living in desperate situations. These people lived in the harsh reality of life in one of the poorer areas of New York City. They were used to all sorts of abuse and suffering: cold, poverty, lack of food, even violence. Jim had told me before the service that many of the women sitting there would stay long after worship was over because they knew the minute they went home their drunken husbands would beat them.

As I looked into their eyes, I realized that my songs just weren't reaching them. They were nice enough—in fact, they were good words—but they didn't relate to where these people were. I just stopped in the middle of my presentation. I turned around and said to someone on the platform, "Do you have a hymnbook?" I was handed an old hymnbook, and I quickly found what I was looking for in the index. Then I faced the crowd and began to sing:

> When peace, like a river, attendeth my way
> When sorrows like sea billows roll;
> Whatever my lot, Thou hast taught me to say,
> "It is well, it is well with my soul."[1]

As the beautiful words of that well-loved hymn fell on the ears of the audience, I could see that all across the church hands began to raise in worship. Some people were on their knees, tears rolling down their faces.

That hymn, written by a man who lost his four daughters and all his possessions in a terrible shipwreck, reminded us again that whatever we face, whatever we go through, whatever changes or does not change, there is still a great truth that all God's people can embrace. Even in the darkness and disillusionment, when dreams are shattered we can sing, "It is well, it is well with my soul."

And I learned again that morning that in any situation Christians always have a better song to sing. Because we have faith in Christ's loving sacrifice, we always have hope.

VAN GOGH WAS MORE THAN A PAINTER

One of my favorite personages from the world of art is the painter Vincent Van Gogh, whose life was dramatized in Irving Stone's novel *Lust for Life*, which was made into a film starring Kirk Douglas. If you read the book or saw the film, you know that Van Gogh was far more than a painter who became a tormented man unable to live in the real world.

Early in his life he was an evangelist, and his mission organization sent him to a region in Belgium where the coal miners lived in desperate poverty. Van Gogh was provided with a nice house, but when he saw the shacks the miners were living in, he found it impossible to live in his much finer quarters.

He probably told himself, *If I'm going to reach them, I'm going to live as one of them.* And so he moved into a horrible shack, wore virtually nothing but a sack, and began to hold meetings. Eventually, people began to come to his meetings, and for six months he had an incredible impact in that area. Unfortunately, the head of his mission board came down for a visit. When he saw how Van Gogh was living— as one of the poor and downtrodden—the man became so disgusted with Van Gogh that he fired him.

Van Gogh had to leave the people he was trying to help,

but they never forgot his sermons, which included statements like: "For those who believe in Jesus Christ, there is no sorrow that is not mixed with hope." And Van Gogh also said: "It's an old belief and a good one that we are strangers on earth, yet we are not alone, for our Father is with us."[3]

FINALLY, OUR EYES MUST SEE ONLY HIM

Psalm 139 is one of my favorite passages because it describes so beautifully how the Lord is always with us—every moment of every day and night. Each time I read this, it strengthens my hope. Hope is realizing that your destiny is interwoven with God's sovereign power and will for your life. As Job went through incredible suffering, he continued to wonder where God was. If only God would make Himself plainly known, then Job would have something to count on, something to keep his hope alive.

Toward the end of the story, God finally appeared in all His sovereign power and glory. After hearing a thunderous barrage of unanswerable questions from the Lord, Job admitted that he had talked about things that he did not understand and that he had spoken of things too wonderful for him to know. Job's confession was Satan's final defeat. The argument between Satan and God that opened the book of Job was settled once and for all because Job now said, "My ears had heard of you before, but *now my eyes have seen you*" (Job 42:5 NCV, italics added).

And then Job added, "So now I hate myself," meaning that he hated his sin, which is what all of us must ultimately hate, no matter what life brings. As Job put it, "I will change my heart and life. I will sit in the dust and ashes"(42:6).

Job had never received an answer to his first question—
"Why?" Nonetheless, it was enough. Even in his pain Job
had found a better song to sing because now he had gained
a new understanding that his only hope was in God.

BLOWN IN HALF, HE BECAME WHOLE

When I think of people God has brought into my life
through my travels or on *Heart to Heart* conversations on
television or in Women of Faith Conferences, I am reminded
a little bit of the "faith hall of fame" listed in chapter 11 of
the book of Hebrews. There are people great and small,
known and unknown, who have had their dreams crushed
and even ground to powder, but they have found hope—and
God's better song.

I remember Bob Wieland, who went to Vietnam standing six feet tall and weighing two hundred and seventy
pounds of rock-hard muscle. Bob came home two feet, ten
and a half inches tall and weighing eighty-seven pounds after
a Viet Cong mine blew him in half.

As Bob talked to me, he described vividly what life was
like for a young American soldier in Vietnam. His graphic
descriptions made me feel the hot, sticky, noisy jungle and
the fear of not knowing what lay around the next clump of
bamboo. Bob told of the day that he and others in his pla-
toon were making their way through the jungle. He could
feel an unnatural stillness, like the tension that builds in you
when you watch a horror movie and you just know that
something is going to jump out and stick a knife between
someone's shoulder blades.

Suddenly Bob heard one of his friends, who was walking

just in front of him, scream. Bob began to run toward him, and that's all he can remember. He stepped on a mine that was big enough to blow away a tank; it threw his upper body one way and his legs another.

After the battle was over, Bob lay there for five days with most of his blood draining out on Vietnamese soil. When medics finally found him, they were sure he was dead, but Bob fooled them. Perhaps he didn't have any legs, but he was still alive and "kicking."

He remembers coming to and thinking, *Well, Lord, they tried to finish me off here, but I'm still alive. So what do You want me to do? What purpose do You have for my life?*

A natural athlete, Bob had planned a professional career in baseball. He now realized that dream was over. Nonetheless, he decided not to lose hope. He would try something else instead. He became a weight lifter and trained day in and day out. Eventually he began competing and made it his new dream to establish a world record.

The big day finally came. Bob gripped three hundred and seventy pounds and with one supreme effort lifted it above his head to establish a new world record.

Before the dust of glory had a chance to settle on Bob's head, he got the news. His title was being taken away. He was disqualified because someone had discovered a rule on the books that said you had to wear shoes while lifting a weight in competition.

As Bob told me this story, I stared in disbelief and blurted, "What did you do? If you didn't snap in Vietnam, surely you had to snap now. You went out there to serve your country; you did what you felt was the right thing; you gave everything you had; and you lost your legs. You came back a different man. You work and train and get to the place where you can break a world record, and they tell you that because you had 'carelessly' left your legs in Vietnam you were disqualified."

Bob smiled and said simply, "What could I do? I looked into the judge's face, shook his hand, and told him, 'I understand. That's all right.'"

Bob Wieland showed me that morning that he grasps something that no book, other than God's Word, can teach: *No earthly crown is ultimately worth anything.* Bob Wieland decided to remember that God is faithful. I imagine that on the day when they took away his medal, in a quiet, unseen place, another jewel of far greater and more infinite value was placed in Bob Wieland's crown.

An Ultra-Marathoner with No Legs!

But Bob wasn't finished. He had a dream to do something for the homeless in America, and he decided that while he didn't have his legs, he did have his hands. He would "walk" across America to raise money for the homeless. Wearing special gloves that were built like shoes, Bob took off, propelling his weight with *nothing but his arms and hands* on a coast-to-coast journey that took three and a half years.

He went through all sorts of weather, discovering support from unlikely people and encountering opposition from others who were embarrassed by his so-called disability. One little eight-year-old boy came up to him and gave him twenty pennies he had in his piggy bank. Homeless people saw him, took out what little change they had, and gave it to him because they understood that he wanted to make a difference.

Everywhere he went, Bob asked God to give him an opportunity to speak to people about the difference that Jesus had made in his life. One day he had traveled mile after mile and had not seen a car, so he asked the Lord, "Before I go to bed tonight, could You just give me two people? Perhaps a car could stop, and I could develop an opportunity to talk to two people about You."

It was almost dusk when a car pulled up beside him and an older couple got out. They talked with Bob for a long time about many things, and eventually Bob said, "Can you see any reason why you shouldn't give your lives to Jesus right now?"

The older couple said they could not, and they joined Bob there on the side of the road, on their knees, and prayed to receive the Lord as their Savior.

But there is one more thing about this story. I'm sure that as Bob lay in bed that night he had a smile on his face. And perhaps there was a tear on his cheek because that older couple whom he had led to the Lord on that dusty road were his own mother and father. Now they also had a better song to sing, because for the first time, they had fixed their hope on Someone who transcends all of life's disappointments and broken dreams.

Our hope in Christ enables us to come to God with open hands into which He can place what He wants and out of which He can take what should not be there.

THERE IS ALWAYS A WAY THROUGH

When the world asks if there is any hope, we can say, "Absolutely!" As Philip Yancey put it, "No one is exempt from tragedy or disappointment—God Himself was not exempt. Jesus offered no immunity, no way *out* of the unfairness, but rather a way *through* it to the other side."[3]

Yancey's words remind me of an illustration Corrie ten Boom used on many occasions. As she spoke, she would hold up the wrong side of a tapestry for her audience to see.

"Isn't this beautiful?" she would ask.

As the people looked at the back of the tapestry, all they saw were threads crossed at odd intervals, knotted in places, looking clumsy and disjointed. It was, to be blunt, ugly.

The audience would stare back at Corrie, not knowing how to respond to her question. Corrie would be silent for a few moments, and then she would say, "Oh! Yes, of course. You can't see the tapestry from my perspective."

Then she would turn the piece of cloth around to show the front, and there would be a picture of a beautiful crown!

At times, life makes no sense. It seems disjointed, distorted, and ugly. But if we surrender our little view of life for God's much grander portrait, we will always be able to hold our eternal hope in Jesus Christ.

13

One Life Does
Make a Difference

───

*When we face our choices, large or small, we can set-
tle for lukewarm, diluted faith. Or we can seek the
real thing, because we know that one life does make
a difference—now and through all eternity.*

I was talking with Sandi Patti and Larnelle Harris
one fall day in 1991 as a coach was taking us to
an evening concert where we were to perform.
Sandi sat up with a shout and pointed out the window. I
scanned the horizon for a three-legged cow, a UFO, a Billy
Graham crusade. But no! Sandi had spotted a Wal-Mart! We
decided Sandi's enthusiasm for Wal-Marts was well shared
across the country, given the $32 billion in business they did
in 1990.

A few months later I sat and listened to the story of Ruth
Glass, a beautifully groomed elegant woman who is the wife
of the CEO of Wal-Mart.

When she was eight years old, Ruth was taken from bar to bar, throughout Albuquerque, New Mexico, by her alcoholic parents. She felt unloved and unlovely. At age fifteen, she married David Glass, hoping that marriage would fill the empty place in her heart.

The young couple struggled financially, sometimes sleeping in their car, sometimes on a mat on a cold floor. But David was a dreamer and was determined to work to realize his dreams.

Together they put David through college. Then one good job begat another. As he became more successful, Ruth's insecurities rose to the surface. Having gained some weight with the birth of her two children, she began to take diet pills that had been prescribed for her by her doctor. Soon she needed more and more. Eventually, she was taking thirty-two pills a day. Ruth realized that she was out of control, so she stopped taking them, going cold turkey, but the emptiness remained. Ruth then began to drink—a glass of wine before she left for an evening, a couple of glasses when she arrived at her destination, and a glass when she came home.

As she sat in her room one afternoon, having drunk all day, David came in and stood over her. He looked her in the face, turned, and left with the children. Ruth knew she had become everything she despised in her parents—an out-of-control drunk.

The afternoon faded into evening, and gradually a plan unfolded in her mind. There was a long, winding cliff-top road near the Glasses' home, and Ruth decided she would drive off it. She would make it look like an accident, of course. David would remarry; the children would have a new mother who would love and care for them; there would be no ugly divorce, no loose ends.

As Ruth told me of her plans to kill herself, I was chilled by her carefully thought-out reasoning. In her mind it was the most loving thing to do.

During the next few days, Ruth stayed in her room, numb to the passage of time. She finally flicked on the television and heard a voice telling her Jesus loved her. Arrested by those words, Ruth cried out for God to save her. She knew this was her last chance to get help. As she prayed, a peace and a joy she had never known began to swell inside her heart. And Ruth knew without a shadow of a doubt that she had come face-to-face with the God of the universe.

Each day after that Ruth Glass sat down with her Bible, a glass of wine, and a cigarette and read and reread the Gospels. She had no idea of how a Christian should live; she just wanted to know more about this Jesus who loved her. One day she noticed after she had been there for hours that the wineglass was still full. God had healed her heart. She didn't need alcohol anymore.

Ruth gave up on herself, and God became her refuge and her strength, a very present help in trouble.

Psalm 46:6–7 says that nations may rage and kingdoms may be moved, but God's voice melts the earth. Nothing can stand against the power of God. He makes wars cease—wars that rage around us and wars of fears and insecurities that rage against our souls. "Be still," the psalmist wrote, "and know that I am God" (v. 10). When we are still, we will see God's works and strength. We will see, just as Ruth Glass did, that God has been with us all along and that He wants to heal us so we can serve Him.

Today Ruth travels the country, telling others of the love of God. Some hide their loneliness behind exquisitely tailored suits, some drown their pain with pills and alcohol. Ruth is able to tell them that God is not a distant, benevolent old man, but He is a very present help in times of trouble.

Ruth's life is making a difference throughout our country. So do our lives every day. And they not only make a difference to those around us; they also make a difference to the Lord.

DO WE HEAR HIM CLAPPING?

Every time I think of Ruth and the difference she is making, I am reminded of a story about a famous conductor who came from Germany to America to lead one of the greatest orchestras ever assembled. It was an incredible performance, and as the final crescendo of music died away, the audience rose to its feet, applauding and cheering. The lone exception was a man in the front row, who remained seated, refusing to clap.

The conductor came off the stage looking distressed, and someone said, "What's wrong? Listen. Listen to the applause! Listen to the cheers!"

"There is one man in the front row who isn't clapping," the conductor said.

"So what?" was the answer. "Listen to everybody else."

"You don't understand," the conductor said sadly. "That man is my teacher. He is the master."

I often ask myself, just as the conductor did, "Who is clapping?" Ruth Glass should be able to see the Lord clapping for her. Certainly I can see Him giving her a big high five.

Yet I need to ask myself the same question: Is the Lord

clapping for me? If He's sitting there in the front row of my life and isn't clapping, it's because I have settled for a watered-down faith when I could have reached out for the real thing.

OUR CHOICES AFFECT GOD AFTER ALL

Undiluted faith is the kind that never forgets that one life does make a difference. Our choices always count. When you read the book of Job, it is not difficult to detect that the wisest words of advice came from Job's younger friend, the angry but sincere Elihu. He made many telling points, to which Job had no reply. While trying to explain God's sovereign greatness, Elihu made what he believed to be a true statement:

> If you sin, it does nothing to God; even if your sins are
> many, they do nothing to him.
> If you are good, you give nothing to God; he receives
> nothing from your hand.
> Your evil ways only hurt a man like yourself,
> and the good you do only helps other human beings.
> (Job 35:6–8 NCV).

Theologians will undoubtedly say that in the final analysis Elihu is right. The God All-Powerful needs nothing to sustain Him. No one would argue that, but in another very real sense Elihu is wrong. As Philip Yancey wrote, "The opening and closing . . . chapters of Job prove that God was greatly affected by the response of one man and that cosmic issues were at stake."[1]

Yancey went on to say that the "wager" between God

and Satan "resolved decisively that the faith of a single human being counts for very much, indeed."[2]

To think otherwise is to fall into Satan's trap and believe that our lives and our actions don't really make a difference. Satan loves it when the Christian sales representative who struggles with pornography reaches one more time for the adult television channel while alone in his hotel room. The devil rejoices when the young woman who's tired of her marriage lies in her husband's arms, dreaming of someone else. And he rubs his hands in glee when the businessperson makes out a tax return that makes it look as if he had a harder year than the prosperous one that he and his family enjoyed.

If our lives don't make a difference and we can do nothing for God, why bother? Who really cares? God is loving and forgiving. We're all human, and the Lord will understand. We can always bail out by saying, "If my life had been easier, I'd have made better choices. I never thought it would be like this."

EVERY RIGHT CHOICE
MAKES HEAVEN SHOUT

When I was a little girl my favorite story was *Peter Pan*. As I watched the movie for the first time, the words of Peter Pan rang in my ears: "Every time a child says, 'I don't believe in fairies,' a fairy dies." Later that night I lay in bed saying over and over, "I do believe in fairies, I do believe in fairies. Of course, I believe in fairies. My dog believes in fairies; my cat believes in fairies; my mum loves fairies."

I have to tell you that today I don't believe in fairies, but I do believe this:

> Every time a believer struggles with sorrow or loneliness or ill health or pain and chooses to trust and serve God anyhow, a bell rings out across heaven and the angels give a great shout. Why? Because one more pilgrim has shown again that he or she understands that Jesus is worth it all. God is faithful.[2]

Life can be hard—and grossly unfair. When the bad things happen, we often ask, "Can I trust God?" But perhaps the real question is, "Can God trust me?" Can He trust us to hold on? Can He trust us to want to become mature Christians, or will we remain little children who believe in Him only if He makes it worth our while? When life seems to cave in for no reason at all, will we remember that God is faithful?

If we're going to be able to handle life when it doesn't seem to make sense, we have to get real. We have to set our faces in the right direction and keep walking as He walked. At times the road will be long and dark, the mountains unscalable. Because we're human we won't always make perfect choices. Sometimes it will seem we take two steps forward and one step back, but it doesn't really matter. *All that really matters is being on the right road.*

THERE IS A NEW EMERGING LEADERSHIP

I was walking through the mall the other evening, flipping through the pages of a new book I had just purchased. I became so interested I almost walked into the tiny wheelchair of a little girl who couldn't have been more than four years old. My heart ached as I looked down at that little child, and I thought, *Lord, how I wish I had the faith of a mustard seed to look into the eyes of this little girl and say, "In the Name of Jesus Christ of Nazareth, rise up and walk!"*

I long to see God's power and glory strewn across people's lives rather than the wreckage and chaos that is so often there. I do believe with all my heart that a new Christian leadership has emerged during the last decade. These people aren't necessarily the ones with household names whose books are given glowing reviews in the magazines. They don't necessarily conduct meetings attended by huge crowds who witness miracles or signs and wonders. Nonetheless, I believe they are a new emerging leadership, because they are people who have been baptized in love, people who have had their hearts broken and who can sing with Isaac Watts:

> To Christ, who won for sinners grace
> By bitter grief and anguish sore,
> Be praise from all the ransomed race
> Forever and forevermore.[3]

You can tell when you're in the company of those who, like Ruth Glass, have been through deep water. They have been through the very valley of the shadow of death, but they have walked every step of the way holding on to Jesus' hand. And they have emerged on the other side with a brighter light, a more tender heart, and a loving, outstretched hand for others.

All around us in the streets of America and across this

world we see devastation. We see people whose lives are broken. We look across to Communist nations and see disillusionment as their Marxist-Leninist regimes have fallen apart and left a gaping void.

What will move in to fill that void? I believe with all my heart that God will so baptize His church in His love that we will want to love and expect nothing in return, that we will daily come before the King of kings and the throne of grace and say:

"Lord Jesus, I can't make it through one more day without You. I just don't have enough love. When I see my reflection in the mirror, I am puzzled because I know the value you have placed on my life. I know that, through the Cross, You have proclaimed to all the world that this is what you think I'm worth. And I wear that proudly, like a new suit of clothes. I want to walk today through a world that has gone sour, bringing the fragrance of Jesus Christ wherever I go and never forgetting that just one life—even my life—can make a difference, today and in the future."

Certainly the Lord has shown me this as I've talked and prayed with the thousands of women who attend the Women of Faith Conferences.

SEEING THE FUTURE

Early in this book I mentioned our desire to know the future ahead of time. I gave some reasons for why I have decided the mystery of the future is part of God's plan. One final reason occurred to me when I took my son Christian, who was about to turn two years old, to Scotland for the first time.

Mum had been planning and dreaming for months. Her sister, Margaret, arranged a big Yea!-you-are-two family party. My brother's son, Dominic, was three, and I had never met him. Our suitcases were jammed to bursting with everything American we thought he'd like.

Aunt Mary, the matriarch of our family, was holding on through failing health to meet the newest "little lamb." It would be a lovely Christmas. When we arrived at Mum's house, packages galore were under her tree.

But God had planned a special one for me. I never expected such a personal gift from Him, certainly not at this time of the year. How could He give me more than all that Christmas celebrates? As a mother I know there is nothing more to give than your son. But into the business of my life as wife, mother, author, speaker, singer, and forty-two-year-old woman, God carved out a little personal time to unwrap a gift in my spirit.

Standing on the Scottish soil on which I was raised, I felt like Job. I felt as if I had come full circle. The grace and mercy that God had poured into my life suddenly overwhelmed me.

I remembered the tears I had shed as a child, not understanding why I had to be the only girl in my class with no dad. I remembered the awkward teenage years, hating my body as it started to develop, feeling embarrassed and unlovable because of my greasy hair and bad skin. I remembered the years of running at full speed for God, trying to impress Him with my manic devotion. I remembered the first few days in that psychiatric ward, feeling hopeless and sad and lost.

Now as I stood at the edge of the cold winter sea, I was wrapped in God's blanket of love. Just ahead of me, running like the wind chasing seagulls, was my two-year-old bundle of grace and joy. Beside me was Barry, my wonderful, loving, funny, kind husband. Tucked into the pockets of my soul were two years of sharing my life with women all across the country and seeing with my own eyes the way that God shines through the broken places of our lives, bringing hope and life. It seemed so kind to be given this gift on my native soil. It made me want to get down on my knees and worship.

I knew then that the moment wouldn't be so sweet if I had known the future at any time along the way. For the agony of past moments of despair made this moment even more miraculous and joyful. The contrast was so great! The moment so glowing. Yes, God is faithful.

> When the road becomes too rough,
> When you're ready to give up,
> When you're crying out for love,
> God is faithful.
>
> When your peace cannot be found,
> He will never let you down.
> You have chosen solid ground.
> God is faithful.[4]

Thirteen Turning Points
We All Face

- Nothing in my hands I bring; simply to Thy cross I cling.

- When life doesn't make sense anymore, we can give up, or we can remember who Jesus really is and that, no matter how dark it gets, He is worth it all.

- When low self-esteem and doubt paralyze us, we can give up and accept this clouded image, or we can remember who we are in Christ.

- When guilt occupies the secret places in our lives, we can let it cripple us, or we can allow God to set us free.

- When the heat of problems and pain burns into our very souls, we can crawl away and hide when it gets too hot, or we can choose to be living sacrifices who stay on the altar for His sake.

- Christian service is a poor substitute for Jesus Himself. We must ask, "Do I want to run myself ragged doing things for God, or do I want the best part—being His friend and knowing Him face-to-face?"

- When this complex, plastic world tries to squeeze us into a designer mold, we can let pride take over, or we can shake free to live the simple truth of the gospel with humility.

- When God seems far away and our prayers bounce off the ceiling, we can give in to despair, or we can keep holding on to heaven in simple trust.

- When we feel weak and overcome, we can wallow in self-pity, or we can choose to reach out and help one another.

- When life is tough, we can give up, or we can come before the Lord with our problem—and wait patiently for His answer.

- When the needy cross our path, we can choose to show selfish indifference, or we can take our eyes off our own needs and follow Jesus to love the unlovely.

- When our dreams seem to go sour or remain unfulfilled, hopelessness can dominate our lives—or we can hold on with open hands, knowing that we have hope because God is faithful.

- When we face our choices, large or small, we can settle for lukewarm, diluted faith—or we can seek the real thing, because we know that one life does make a difference now and through all eternity.

NOTES

CHAPTER 1

1. Chris Eaton, "God Is Faithful." Lyrics reproduced courtesy of Clouseau Music/SGO Music Publishing Ltd.

CHAPTER 2

1. John Fischer, *True Believers Don't Ask Why* (Minneapolis: Bethany House, 1989), 19.
2. Ibid., 19.
3. Hannah Whitall Smith as quoted by Mary W. Tyleston, *Daily Strength for Daily Needs* (London: Methuan & Co., 1922).

CHAPTER 4

1. Phil McHugh, "In Heaven's Eyes." Copyright © 1985, River Oaks Music Co. Used by permission.
2. Al Kasha and Joel Hirschhorn, *Reaching the Morning After* (Nashville: Thomas Nelson, 1986), 13.
3. Ibid., 153.
4. Al Kasha, "The Morning After." Copyright © 1972, W. B. Music Corp. and Warner-Tamerlane Publishing Co. Used by permission.

CHAPTER 7

1. Ron Trott and Jon Sweet, "Sand in the Hand." Copyright © 1986, Swot Patch Music. Used by permission.

2. Sheila Walsh, Greg Nelson, and Bob Farrell, "Come into His Kingdom." Copyright © 1989, Word Music, Summerdawn Music/Greg Nelson Music. Used by permission.

3. Sheila Walsh, "It Could Have Been Me." Copyright © 1990, Word Music. Used by permission.

4. Ibid.

CHAPTER 8

1. David Biebel, *If God Is So Good, Why Do I Hurt So Bad?* (Ada, MI: Revell, 1995).

2. Ibid.

3. Rebecca Manley Pippert, *Hope Has Its Reasons* (New York: Harper and Row, 1989).

CHAPTER 11

1. Ron Trott, Sheila Walsh, and Jon Sweet, "Angels with Dirty Faces." Copyright © 1986, Swot Patch Music. Used by permission.

CHAPTER 12

1. These words are from "It Is Well with My Soul" by Horatio G. Spafford, 1828–1888, altered.

2. Irving Stone, *Lust for Life* (New York: Doubleday, 1934).

3. Philip Yancey, *Disappointment with God* (Grand Rapids: Zondervan, 1988), 186.

CHAPTER 13

1. Yancey, *Disappointment with God*, 170.

2. Ibid., 170.

3. The fifth, but seldom printed, stanza to Isaac Watts's well-known hymn "When I Survey the Wondrous Cross."

4. Chris Eaton, "God Is Faithful." Lyrics reproduced courtesy of Clouseau Music/SGO Music Publishing Ltd.

A BIBLE STUDY

Guide

FOR THIS BOOK
AND THE BOOK OF JOB

INTRODUCTION

══

When times are tough and everything is against us, our natural inclination is to ask, "Where is God? Will He protect me? Is He trustworthy? Can I believe His promises?"

In this book and study guide, Sheila Walsh answers these questions with a resounding "Yes!"

Life Is Tough but God Is Faithful takes you into the hearts of those who have discovered how to triumph in spite of suffering. Sheila offers insights from the book of Job to identify crucial choices from her own experience and the experiences of many other Christians who have discovered God's faithfulness in their own troubles and sorrows.

Life Is Tough but God Is Faithful is an encouraging look at who God is and how much He loves us—and how He wants to work with us in our choices. This heartfelt look at our attitudes in tough times is a ringing affirmation of God's love, power, and forgiveness.

Sheila says, "Undiluted faith is the kind that never forgets that one life does make a difference. Our choices always count . . . I want to walk today through a world that has gone sour, bringing the fragrance of Jesus Christ wherever I go and never forgetting that just one life—even my life—can make a difference, today and in the future."

MANY DIFFERENT USES

There are many different ways to effectively use this material:

Private Study: You will discover that personal study can be highly rewarding and profitable.

Weekly Small Groups: The advantage of this approach is the additional time allowed between meetings for study and reflection. The sessions are formatted so that each one covers a chapter of the book. Homework for each session is to read the next chapter.

Retreat Setting: Count on needing at least eight to nine hours of group time. With a Friday night and Saturday schedule, you'll be away from distractions and gathered in a very productive setting. The *Life Is Tough but God Is Faithful* video will make your retreat experience even more beneficial. You might also consider playing the song "God Is Faithful" from Sheila's *Hope* album.

Sunday School: You'll discover that this study guide, along with the video, is a natural for Sunday school or adult Bible study classes.

You may be using this guide for your own personal study. Or you may be conducting a group Bible study, Sunday school class, or retreat. If so, the Facilitator's Introduction, which is next, will help you in this process.

As Christians, we all desire to grow stronger in our faith

and obtain a deeper understanding of God. We pray that this study material will help you accomplish some of these goals in your own Christian journey.

FACILITATOR'S
INTRODUCTION

═══

T his facilitator's introduction is meant to serve as a guidepost. You can use it in great detail or take a slightly different path—it's your choice. The guide is easy to use and gives you flexibility to adapt to the needs of your students.

Study Questions: The answers to questions in the Study Guide appear at the end of each session.

Video: This study guide can be supplemented by the *Life Is Tough but God Is Faithful* video. You can purchase this video directly from Sheila Walsh's Web site: sheilawalsh.com. The video can enrich your study experience, since Sheila herself becomes a part of your group.

The video is divided into four sessions, but for the purpose of this study, you will want to divide these sessions into smaller parts. The Facilitator Suggestions throughout this guide will provide ways to do this. (You won't always be using the sessions in the order they appear on the video.) There is material on the video that is not in the book; therefore, the video is a further enrichment of this program.

Other Materials: At certain times in the study, other

enrichment materials are mentioned: Sheila's album, *Hope*, which has the song "God Is Faithful" on it. And also Sheila's book, *Stories from the River of Mercy*, which chronicles the journey of Sheila and her mother-in-law as they found grace and mercy in the deep blue waters of Eleanor's illness.

SUGGESTIONS FOR EFFECTIVE USE

Preview all Scripture references: Since this is a Bible study, it is recommended that you become familiar with passages before each group session.

Have ample supplies on hand: Always have extra pencils and paper on hand. Each person in the group should have a copy of this book.

Be sensitive to staying on schedule: Start and end on time. Avoid rabbit trails by steering students to new questions.

Get people involved: Don't allow one or two individuals to do all the talking. If needed, call on specific students for greater group participation.

Don't be afraid of silence: As a facilitator, even a few seconds of silence can seem long. Don't panic. Wait and if no one answers, rephrase the question, or call on someone directly. Avoid answering your own questions.

Be affirming: Remember, there are no dumb questions or answers. Be affirming, even if the answers you receive are not what you expect. Communicate how much you appreciate every answer.

Pray: Pray for your group members before each session.

Preview each video: If you use the video, preview the entire tape before beginning this study. Then preview the particular portion for each group session, taking any notes in your copy of this book. (Suggestions for portions for certain sessions are made throughout the study guide.)

Agree to have a code of secrecy: Hopefully, the Bible study group you are forming will become a true circle of friends. (Or if your group has been in existence before, the trust within your fellowship will increase.) For this relationship to build, the members must agree that what is discussed in the group will not be mentioned in other circles.

INITIAL SESSION

You might want to have an initial get-together, during which you could give participants their copies of this book and encourage them to read the first chapter before the next session. If you do so, you might want to begin this session with Session 1 of the video. During this part Sheila welcomes the participants, prays with them, and then introduces the questions women have asked her at Women of Faith conferences. Stop the video at the point where the book is pictured; this is where you will begin the next session.

This initial one-hour session can also be used for the women to get acquainted with each other and to begin to pray together. Refreshments would set a friendly environment for group participation.

SESSION 1

Nothing in my hands I bring; simply to Thy cross I cling.

CHAPTER 1:
THE WHOLE POINT

*I*ntroduction: *On tour with the Women of Faith conferences, Sheila has met many women who have shared their stories and how God has worked in their lives. However, many have questions about why God has let them suffer. Questions like:*

- *If God loves me, why did my child die?*

- *If God loves me, why am I forty-three years old and still single? I have done everything to honor the Lord with my life, so why am I living my life alone?*

- *If God loves me, why didn't He heal my husband of cancer?*

1. Have you ever asked questions like these? Have you ever wondered, *God, if You are so good, why am I having such a hard time?* Describe these times in your life:

2. Do you ever question whether your prayers are answered? _____ Why?

3. Have you ever felt abandoned by God? _____ When?

4. Have you ever been surprised at going through a difficult trial at a time when you thought you were doing everything right for God? _____ How did you respond?

5. Consider the following Scripture passage:

There was a man in the land of Uz, whose name was Job; and that man was blameless and upright, and one who feared God and shunned evil. And seven sons and three daughters were born to him. Also, his possessions were seven thousand sheep, three thousand camels, five hundred yoke of oxen, five hundred female donkeys, and a very large household, so that this man was the greatest of all the people of the East.

And his sons would go and feast in their houses, each on his appointed day, and would send and invite their three sisters to eat and drink with them.

So it was, when the days of feasting had run their course, that Job would send and sanctify them, and he would rise early in the morning and offer burnt offerings according to the number of them all. For Job said, "It may be that my sons have sinned and cursed God in their hearts." Thus Job did regularly.

Now there was a day when the sons of God came to present themselves before the LORD, and Satan also came among them.

And the LORD said to Satan, "From where do you come?" So Satan answered the LORD and said, "From going to and fro on the earth, and from walking back and forth on it."

Then the LORD said to Satan, "Have you considered My servant Job, that there is none like him on the earth, a blameless and upright man, one who fears God and shuns evil?"

So Satan answered the LORD and said, "Does Job fear God for nothing?

"Have You not made a hedge around him, around his household, and around all that he has on every side? You have blessed the work of his hands, and his possessions have increased in the land.

"But now, stretch out Your hand and touch all that he has, and he will surely curse You to Your face!"

And the LORD *said to Satan, "Behold, all that he has*
is in your power; only do not lay a hand on his person."

Job 1:1–12

6. Why do you think God turned his servant Job over to Satan?

7. Have you ever felt as if God has turned you over to suffer? Describe the time:

8. If God's purpose for our lives on this earth is not peace and rest, what is it?

ANSWERS TO QUESTIONS

Question 1: God had something important to teach Job. One reason God allows His children to suffer is to produce fruit. If we allow suffering to accomplish its purpose, it can bring forth patience (Hebrews 10:36, James 1:3), joy (Psalm 30:5, Psalm 126:6), knowledge (Psalm 94:12), and maturity (1 Peter 5:10).

Question 8: To become more like Him.

Facilitator Suggestions

If you did not have an initial meeting and want to use the video, start Session 1 of the video at the beginning of this session and play until Session 1 ends. Sheila suggests that the group members write down their disappointments and questions (an exercise we will do later in this study). Explain to your members that you will be doing this in a later session. If you did have an initial meeting, start the video where you left off (at the picture of the book) and continue until the end of Session 1.

The song that is quoted in this chapter, "God Is Faithful," is found on Sheila's album *Hope*. You might want to purchase this album at a Christian bookstore or on Sheila's Web site (sheilawalsh.com) and play the song as an ending to this session.

Assignment for next session:
Read Chapter 2.

SESSION 2

TURNING POINT

When life doesn't make sense anymore, we can give up, or we can remember who Jesus really is and that no matter how dark it gets, He is worth it all.

CHAPTER 2:
IT WASN'T SUPPOSED TO BE THIS WAY

When Darrell Gilyard was fourteen, he found himself out on the streets. He had no name, no family he knew, no one who cared if he lived or died. He made his bed under a bridge, selling cans and bottles to make enough to eat. He kept going to school, washing his one set of clothes in the river. At night he would sit under the light of a convenience store to do his homework. He was determined not to be a loser.

But there were plenty of cold nights when he lifted his face to the sky and asked God why. Certainly life had been *unfair to him, and he had little reason to believe that God is faithful.*

1. If some people find it difficult to believe that "life is tough, but God is faithful," then what do they believe?

2. What did Sheila question during Eleanor's fight with cancer?

3. When bad things occur in your life, do you wonder, *Is God angry with me?* or *Have I done something wrong?* Give an example:

4. How do you personally resolve this tough question of "Is God angry with me?" in your own mind?

5. Consider this Scripture passage.

> *Again there was a day when the sons of God came to present themselves before the* LORD, *and Satan came also among them to present himself before the* LORD.

And the L*ORD* *said to Satan, "From where do you come?" So Satan answered the* L*ORD* *and said, "From going to and fro on the earth, and from walking back and forth on it."*

Then the L*ORD* *said to Satan, "Have you considered My servant Job, that there is none like him on the earth, a blameless and upright man, one who fears God and shuns evil? And still he holds fast to his integrity, although you incited Me against Him, to destroy him without cause."*

So Satan answered the L*ORD* *and said, "Skin for skin! Yes, all that a man has he will give for his life.*

"But stretch out Your hand now, and touch his bone and his flesh, and he will surely curse You to Your face!"

And the L*ORD* *said to Satan, "Behold, he is in your hand, but spare his life."*

Job 2:1–6

6. Why did God allow Satan to assault Job again?

7. Has your experience been similar to the old adage "Trouble comes in threes"? _____

8. Why do we tend to think that if we believe in God, our lives will always be painless?

ANSWERS TO QUESTIONS

Question 1: Many think of God in terms of their present circumstances. They think that if life is tough, then God must be unfaithful. (Or if life is going well, then God is faithful.)

But Darrell Gilyard did not give in to this mistaken belief. As he struggled to survive, all he had was Jesus. He decided that he had to take his eyes off his circumstances and focus them on the Lord. Time passed, and nothing changed. Although Darrell was laughed at and ridiculed, his perspective on life changed, and he experienced overwhelming peace and contentment.

Question 2: Why God didn't heal her.

Question 6: Another reason God allows suffering is to silence the devil. Satan once accused Job of merely serving God for the material blessings involved. But the Lord allowed the devil to torment Job to demonstrate that His servant loved God because of who He was, not for what he could get from Him.

FACILITATOR SUGGESTIONS

Have the group read through the entire second chapter of Job, which introduces Job's friends.

If you are using the video, ask the group members to make a list of the things that they think make God love them and bring the list next time. (Obviously, this is flawed theology, which Sheila points out in the video in Session 3.)

ASSIGNMENT FOR NEXT SESSION:
Read Chapter 3.

SESSION 3

TURNING POINT
When low self-esteem and doubt paralyze us, we can give up and accept this clouded image, or we can remember who we are in Christ.

CHAPTER 3:
CLOUDED IMAGES

*I*ntroduction: Sheila's dad suffered a thrombosis in his brain and was never completely sane again. At times he suffered "brain storms," which put him into a rage and gave him the strength of three men. One day when Sheila was four, her dad came toward her with a strange look in his eyes. He raised his cane and at that moment Sheila knew that he was going to hit her. Quickly she pulled the cane away from him, and he lost his balance and fell. He lay there moaning, and Sheila was sure it was all her fault.

As she grew older, she felt that God held her responsible for this; she believed that He couldn't love her.

1. Did God really stop loving Sheila or Job? _____ Do you find it difficult to believe that God still loves you, no matter what you have done? _____

2. How do you resolve such doubts?

As the years went by, Sheila was unable to pray to God as Father. She admits, "I was trying to bury my dad's tragedy deep inside. I blotted out that horrible night when they took my dad to the psychiatric hospital, and I substituted my own fantasy. My father and I were walking along the beach and suddenly he was "taken home." There was no pain or screaming or fear.

3. Counselors believe that our image of God can often be impaired by our relationship with our fathers. Do you avoid calling God "Father" when you pray? _____ If so, why?

4. Has your relationship with your father affected your relationship with God? _____ If so, how?

5. Has your relationship with your parents affected your self-esteem? _____ If so, how?

6. Consider the following Scripture:

For You formed my inward parts;
You covered me in my mother's womb.

I will praise You, for I am fearfully and wonderfully made;
Marvelous are Your works,
And that my soul knows very well.

Psalm 139:13–14

7. Since you are fearfully and wonderfully made by God, what does this truth imply about your value as a person?

8. Take a few minutes and create a movie in your mind of your own life. Now, list the images that came to mind for your movie.

9. Why were these points in your life so important that your mind would flash back to them?

10. What is clearly the most important time or event?

11. Now, write down what you think God sees when He reviews your life.

12. Are there differences in your answers to questions 10 and 11? _____ If so, why?

13. Were there points of disappointment or mistakes in your movie? List them below.

14. Do you think God still loves you, despite your mistakes? _____ Whatever your answer, consider these words

of inspiration, which Sheila mentioned in Chapter 2 and have been so important to her through the years:

> *Put together all the tenderest love you know,*
> *The deepest you have ever felt,*
> *And the strongest that has ever been poured out upon you,*
> *And heap upon it all the love of all the loving human*
>   *hearts in the world,*
> *And then multiply it by infinity,*
> *And you will begin, perhaps,*
> *To have some faint glimpse of the love God has for you.*
>   *—Hannah Whitall Smith*

15. Write a letter to God. Express how you feel and where you are in your life. Remember, this is between you and God—you don't have to share this letter with anyone. So, be completely open and honest.

ASSIGNMENT FOR NEXT SESSION:
Read Chapter 4.

FACILITATOR'S SUGGESTIONS

If you are using the video, skip to Session 4 and use the material at the beginning of this session. Stop the video at the point where Sheila begins to talk about places to hide. (You will use the part about her hospitalization in a later session.)

SESSION 4

TURNING POINT
When guilt occupies the secret places in our lives, we can let it cripple us, or we can allow God to set us free.

CHAPTER 4:
NO HIDDEN PLACES

*I*ntroduction: *Sheila was troubled by guilt for much of her teenage and college years.* Had I caused my father's death? *she wondered.* Had I made him hate me? *I had never been sure, and the best way I could cope with growing up was to bottle it up inside.*

1. What have you bottled up in a secret place inside yourself?

2. As Sheila looked back on her college years, she saw that part of her motivation for serving God was to prove to God that she was worthy of His love. Are you driving yourself like this? _____ How?

3. Then during morning chapel, the speaker spoke from Isaiah 43:18–19:

> *Do not remember the former things,*
> *Nor consider the things of old.*
> *Behold, I will do a new thing,*
> *Now it shall spring forth;*
> *Shall you not know it?*

Verses 18 and 19 burned into her memory. Later, as she prayed with a friend, she realized that she had rarely called God "Father" (the first time this occurred to her). Now she understood why. The pain caused by her own father's death had been too much to bear, and she didn't want to link God with that.

Read these verses about God as Father and claim them for yourself: Romans 8:15–17 and 2 Corinthians 6:18.

The next day Sheila went home to see her mother. Together they walked through those difficult years of Sheila's dad's illness. That weekend of reminiscing changed those memories. "The fear and guilt that had festered inside me ever since I was four years old was beginning to cleanse away. I realized that what had happened to my dad was not his fault—and it certainly was not mine. I finally understood that pulling away his cane and making him fall was not an unforgivable sin, but only the act of a frightened little girl who couldn't understand what had happened to her dad."

4. Take a moment now and pray to God as your Father. Picture Him in the center of that secret place and feel Him restore those moments.

5. Read the story of the Samaritan woman in John 4:1–26. How are you like her?

6. Jesus revealed the woman's hidden secret. But His compassionate words also made her realize that she didn't have to run anymore. He knew it all, and yet He loved her. Are you willing to be set free by the healing light of God's love?

FACILITATOR SUGGESTIONS

Consider using Sheila's book *Stories from the River of Mercy* as a resource for this session. This book walks through the relationship between Sheila and her mother-in-law, a relationship that was healed during Eleanor's illness. (You can purchase it from your local Christian bookstore or from Sheila's Web site: sheilawalsh.com.)

This session is about hidden secrets. You might ask the

group to think about the hidden secrets in their lives. Then read to them a portion of the "Broken Dreams and Unexpected Graces" essay, beginning at the bottom of page 85: "The next day Christian wanted to take a nap . . ."

Ask the group how important these hidden places seem to be in relation to the totality of their lives—the moment when they came into this world and the moment when we are so close to home, we are once again helpless and dependent. Isn't this the perspective we need to have as we consider the difficult times in our lives?

ASSIGNMENT FOR NEXT SESSION:
Read Chapter 5.

SESSION 5

TURNING POINT
When the heat of problems and pain burns into our very souls, we can crawl away and hide when it gets too hot, or we can choose to be living sacrifices who stay on the altar for His sake.

CHAPTER 5:
LIVING SACRIFICES DON'T CRAWL AWAY

*I*ntroduction: *When Sheila first met Joni Eareckson Tada, she couldn't understand how Joni could be happy confined to a wheelchair. Then, one day after a conference, Joni shared that she was better off than Sheila—even though she was paralyzed. Sheila didn't understand. Joni explained—she could never forget that she was handicapped, but Sheila can and does forget. The truth is, we are all handicapped. However, the fact that Joni still suffers pain in her neck caused Sheila to question God—how could God* *allow Joni to suffer more? She asked God to give her a passage—and He gave her 1 Peter 1:6–9:*

> *In this you greatly rejoice, though now for a little while, if need be, you have been grieved by various trials, that the genuineness of your faith, being much more precious than gold that perishes, though it is tested by fire, may be found to praise, honor, and glory at the revelation of Jesus Christ, whom having not seen, you love. Though now you do not see Him, yet believing, you rejoice with joy inexpressible and full of glory, receiving the end of your faith—the salvation of your souls.*

1. What timeless truth did Sheila learn from Joni's suffering and 1 Peter 1: 6–9?

2. Do you ever feel angry at God during the difficult times? Explain past experiences.

3. Consider the following Scripture:

> *I beseech you therefore, brethren, by the mercies of God, that you present your bodies a living sacrifice, holy, acceptable to God, which is your reasonable service.*
>
> *Romans 12:1*

What is unique about a living sacrifice?

Sheila admits: "The more I walk with the Lord, the more I understand that every day of my life, for the rest of my walk on this earth, I can choose to stay on the altar or to crawl away. When the heat is turned up, I can crawl off and say, 'Well, this is not what I signed up for. I thought that this would make me feel good. I thought that all my prayers would be answered, but it seems as if God has turned a deaf ear to my cry.'"

4. Can you remember specific times you placed certain areas of your life on the altar only to retrieve them again? _____ Explain:

5. Why is it so hard to keep our lives on the altar? Is it a matter of trusting God? What do you think?

6. During trials and suffering, do you find it difficult to look beyond the present and into the future? _____ List practical

ideas to help remind you of these truths in future times of suffering:

7. _____ is definitely a better teacher than all our joyful moments in life. We are changed _____ through _____.

ANSWERS TO QUESTIONS

Question 1: Our reward is not here on earth, but in heaven.

Question 3: A living sacrifice always wants to jump off the altar.

Question 7: <u>Suffering</u> is definitely a better teacher than all our joyful moments in life. We are changed <u>eternally</u> through <u>suffering.</u>

FACILITATOR SUGGESTIONS

If you are using the video, start this session by using a specific part of Session 2. About midway through Session 2 of the video, Sheila talks about Joni Eareckson Tada. ("One of my dearest friends in the world is Joni Eareckson Tada.") Start the video there and go through to the end of Session 2. (Sheila reads 1 Peter 1:4–7 from the *New International Version* on the video, rather than 1 Peter 1:6–9, which is quoted in the book.)

SESSION 6

TURNING POINT
Christian service is a poor substitute for Jesus Himself. We must ask, "Do I want to run myself ragged doing things for God, or do I want the best part—being His friend and knowing Him face-to-face?"

CHAPTER 6:
BE GOD'S FRIEND, NOT JUST HIS SERVANT

*I*ntroduction: *Years ago Sheila worked for the BBC and became frustrated at not being able to speak her heart on the program, so she decided to tour and spread the gospel in person. However, a week before the tour began, Sheila lost her voice. She prayed and went to the doctor— but her voice got worse. She went to see a specialist and found out she had growths on her vocal cords, which prohibited her from speaking for a month—and maybe from ever being able to sing again. The tour was cancelled. "Why did this happen?" she asked God.*

1. What was the important message God spoke to Sheila's heart during this trial?

2. In your own words, describe what you think it means to be a friend to God:

3. List practical ways you can be a friend to God in your daily life:

4. We all know that God is pleased when our faith is shown through good works. But what does God also care about greatly?

5. Take time to evaluate and write down things that you think God really likes about you.

6. List practical ways you can start spending more time with God:

ANSWERS TO QUESTIONS

Question 1: God has many servants, but few friends.

Question 4: God cares about us and our relationship with Him.

FACILITATOR SUGGESTIONS

If you are using the video, begin where you left off last session—with Sheila telling about her throat problem when she worked at the BBC. ("I used to work in England on the BBC.") Go through until the end of Session 3.

ASSIGNMENT FOR NEXT SESSION:
Read Chapter 7.

SESSION 7

When this complex, plastic world tries to squeeze us into a designer mold, we can let pride take over, or we can shake free to live the simple truth of the gospel with humility.

CHAPTER 7:
KEEPING IT SIMPLE KEEPS IT REAL

Introduction: Sheila was deeply affected by the PTL scandal and Christians' reaction to it. "Why are we so cruel to one another?" she asked herself. "Why do we hit out so violently when someone crumbles?"

She knew that sin should be dealt with, but she was disappointed by the spectators who find it so much easier to believe the worst than to hold on to the best. And long before the PTL scandal, she felt the Lord was gently dealing with her own overconfidence. She felt strongly:

It could have been me.
I could have been the one to lose my grip and fall.

It could have been me,
The one who takes such subtle pride in always standing
    tall.
For unless You hold me tightly, Lord, and I can hold on,
    too,
Then tomorrow in the news it could be me . . .

From "It Could Have Been Me" by Sheila Walsh. Copyright © 1990 Word Music. Used by permission.

1. Could it be you? _____ Do you sometimes tend to take pride in your accomplishments or your spirituality? _____ When?

2. The apostles also had difficulties with their pride. Consider, for instance, James and John, who asked Jesus if they could sit at His right and left in heaven (Mark 10:35–45). Yet history bears out that they were not able to stand when Jesus stood. How can you avoid pride, which is often said to be the greatest sin of all?

3. Sheila has also been caught by this sin. She was able to minister to Cindy, a teenager dying of leukemia, but three weeks later when Jennifer, a young woman suffering from

bulimia and depression, called, Sheila hesitated and then tried to end the call quickly (see pages 91–99). What did she learn from this experience?

4. How can you apply this to your own life?

5. The apostle Peter also bought into Satan's lie: "You're not like everybody else. You're strong. It'll never happen to you." Read Matthew 26, verses 31–35 and verses 69–75 to see his failure.

6. What happened to Peter after Jesus' resurrection? Read John 21:1–19.

Answers to Questions

Question 2: Take a healthy assessment of your weaknesses as well as your strengths. Admit that you are not able to stand without Jesus.

Question 3: She learned that she was human; she couldn't be there for everyone. But she could let God hold up a mirror before her face so that she could see the stark reality of who she was. If she had been honest enough to tell her secretary, "I'm tired, and I have several things to do before I can go home. Can you get one of our phone counselors involved?" she would not have been put in this predicament. Or she could have been honest enough to say, "Lord, I don't want to make this call. I want to go home, but someone needs my help, so I need Yours. Please give me Your love and help me to communicate it."

Question 6: Despite Peter's failures, Jesus gave him another chance, just as He does for you and me. And He also gave Peter an even greater responsibility: "Take care of My sheep."

FACILITATOR SUGGESTIONS

If you have purchased *Stories from the River of Mercy,* you might want to read the essay "The Rehearsal Dinner" (page 25). Pride can often pop up in the most important moments, like wedding celebrations. And Sheila and her mother-in-law were no exception.

ASSIGNMENT FOR NEXT SESSION:
Read Chapter 8.

SESSION 8

TURNING POINT
When God seems far away and our prayers bounce off the ceiling, we can give in to despair, or we can keep holding on to heaven in simple trust.

CHAPTER 8:
WHEN ALL OF HEAVEN IS SILENT

*I*ntroduction: *Sheila shares an experience with Debbie, a young woman with multiple sclerosis who frequently watched the PTL program. At times, Debbie felt frustrated with the show because people always talked of healing, but no one ever talked about dying. The young woman had tried to pray for healing, but it never came.*

1. What did Sheila learn from this suffering woman?

2. Can you relate to Debbie's answer? _____ If so, explain.

3. Why do you think people feel closer to God in times of suffering?

4. Many times people aren't healed after they pray for a healing like Debbie did. Certainly Job wasn't healed. Look at his prayer in Job 30:20–23:

> I cry out to You,
>   but You do not answer me;
> I stand up, and You regard me.
> But You have become cruel to me;
> With the strength of Your hand
>   You oppose me.
> You lift me up to the wind
>   and cause me to ride on it;
> You spoil my success.
> For I know that You will bring me to death,
> And to the house appointed for all living.

5. Job's life was devastated. He could not understand why heaven was silent. God did not offer Job any _____ for his suffering.

6. Why do you think God is sometimes silent in times of suffering?

7. Describe the importance of prayer in your life:

8. Rate your prayer life on a scale of 1–10:

9. List the reasons you rated your prayer life as you did.

ANSWERS TO QUESTIONS

Question 1: When Debbie was suffering the most, she felt the closest to God.

Question 5: God did not offer Job any <u>explanation</u> for his suffering.

Question 6: Through suffering, God can deepen our walk with Him.

FACILITATOR SUGGESTIONS

If you are using the video, begin this session with the beginning of Session 2 and play through until Sheila begins talking about Joni Eareckson Tada. ("One of my dearest friends in the world is Joni Eareckson Tada.")

If you don't have the video but do have *Stories from the River of Mercy*, you might read the essay "Compassion: The Child of Joy and Sorrows" (page 90), which talks about the blessings that Eleanor and Sheila received during Eleanor's last days.

SESSION 9

TURNING POINT
When we feel weak and overcome, we can wallow in self-pity, or we can choose to reach out and help one another.

CHAPTER 9:
A CIRCLE OF FRIENDS

*I*ntroduction: Sheila had a friend who joined Alcoholics Anonymous after struggling for a long time on his own and getting nowhere. Yet, after his first AA meeting, he described his experience to her: "I stood up, told them my name, told them I had a problem, and they understood and accepted me. The room was filled with people who knew they couldn't make it on their own. We needed each other . . . For the first time in my life, I realized what the church could be."

The world, Sheila says, is not looking for Stepford-type Christians. The world is looking for real people who admit their failures and share their problems together.

1. When we hide our sins and cover our weaknesses, when we pretend to be Christian supermen and women, we live in denial—"the truth is not in us." And we become isolated from one another and from God.

Have you ever felt the freedom to confess your sins to another Christian? _____ Certainly Job felt this way. He confessed to God in the presence of friends:

> *I have heard of You by the hearing of the ear,*
> *But now my eye sees You.*
> *Therefore I abhor myself,*
> *And repent in dust and ashes.*
>
> *Job 42: 5–6*

2. Do you belong to a group (a circle of friends) that is free to share their problems and their weaknesses with one another? _____ If not, where can you find such a group? Or how can your present study group be more open with one another?

3. The model of our relationship to each other can be found in Jesus' relationship to His disciples at the Last Supper. Read John 13:1–17. What do you think the Lord calls us to do in this passage?

4. What can you do in the days ahead to serve another person?

5. By the time Sheila's father died, his illness had so altered his personality, Sheila thought he did not love her. She was determined not to lose God's love as she had lost her father's love. Thus, she set out to be a perfect Christian. She followed a narrow path as a child, went to seminary to learn how to please God and keep His love, and cohosted the *700 Club*. Yet, she sank into depression.

What did Sheila learn from the depths of her depression?

6. What lessons can you apply to your own life from Sheila's experience?

7. In 1992, Sheila had a breakdown and was placed in the care of a psychiatric hospital. She panicked because her father had died in a psychiatric hospital. The psychiatrist asked Sheila, "Who are you?" It took Sheila a while to answer that question . . .

What important lesson did God show Sheila in the hospital?

8. What lesson did God teach Job?

ANSWERS TO QUESTIONS

Question 2: Hopefully by joining a small group in a church.

Question 3: Some Christians feel called to wash other Christians' feet as a way of showing love to them. But not everyone does. Some show their love by serving their brothers and sisters in Christ.

Question 5: Sheila realized that God didn't just want to her to survive; He wanted her to live to the fullest.

Question 7: All other identities are fleeting and not important in relation to our identity in God.

Question 8: God loved Job for himself.

FACILITATOR SUGGESTIONS

If you are using the video, you will want to go to Session 4 and begin where Sheila talks about places to hide. Play through the video until the psychiatrist asks Sheila as she is leaving the hospital, "Who are you?" and she replies "Sheila Walsh, child of the King of kings."

You may want to divide this session into two sessions, since the material covered here is so extensive.

ASSIGNMENT FOR NEXT SESSION:
Read Chapter 10.

SESSION 10

TURNING POINT
When life is tough, we can give up, or we can come before the Lord with our problem—and wait patiently for His answer.

CHAPTER 10:
IS HEAVEN REALLY SILENT?

*I*ntroduction: One Sunday when Sheila was in the hospital, she went to church with one of the nurses. The pastor said, "Some of you in here feel as if you are dead inside. Christ is here in all His resurrection power. If you will simply call on Him, He will reach into that place and pull you out."

Sheila felt compelled to go to the altar. "For the first time," she said, "I went to God empty-handed. Before, I'd always gone with a new book or a new record or a new something I'd done to make God love me. I finally gave up."

1. Have you ever given complete control of your life to God in this way?_____ If not, what holds you back?

2. Job finally gave God control of his life. He admitted, "I am nothing—how could I ever find the answers? I lay my hand upon my mouth in silence. I have said too much already."

Then he went on to say: "I know that you can do anything and that no one can stop you. You ask who it is who has so foolishly denied your providence. It is I. I was talking about things I knew nothing about and did not understand, things far too wonderful for me" (Job 40:4–5; 42:2–3, TLB). Can you make the same statement to God right now? _____ Write your confession in the space below:

3. Then Job needed to forgive his three friends—Eliphaz, Bildad, and Zophar. Have you truly forgiven people who have harmed you?_____

If not, why?

4. Make a list of those you need to forgive:

5. Pray now that God will help you to forgive them.

6. Write a letter to one person you are forgiving, just as Sheila did. You might mail the letter to the person, but that is not essential as long as you feel true forgiveness in your heart.

FACILITATOR SUGGESTIONS

If you are using the video, go to Session 4 and begin where Sheila says, "I remember the last Sunday I was in the hospital." Stop the video right before Sheila says, "I saw that happening to my dear mother-in-law."

SESSION 11

TURNING POINT

When the needy cross our path, we can choose to show selfish indifference, or we can take our eyes off our own needs and follow Jesus to love the unlovely.

CHAPTER 11:
GOD HAS LEFT US A JOB TO DO

Introduction: In January of 1988 Sheila went to Manila to film a TV documentary about the work of Compassion International, a Christian child sponsorship agency. At the end of this time, she decided to sponsor Belinda, and someone suggested that she meet Belinda's family. The child's home (a one-room shack occupied by her mom and nine siblings) was built over a swamp, and the stench from the open sewers was almost unbearable.

However, the love in this home astounded Sheila. She truly felt what Belinda's mother said: "The Lord's presence fills my home, and His glory is with us."

1. Have you reached out in compassion as Sheila did that day? _____ When?

2. How about Job's three friends? Did they reach out to Job with compassion?_____ What did they do that was wrong? Look at Job, chapter 4 for Eliphaz's comments. Look at Job, chapter 8 for Bildad's comments. Then see Job 11 for Zophar's comments.

3. Do you commit to avoid these errors as you encounter angels with dirty faces or friends who need your support? _____

4. If Job's friends did not show compassion, what is compassion?

5. How did Job respond to this question? (See Job 16:5 in *The Living Bible*.)

6. Is there someone in your church or neighborhood who needs your compassion? List some possibilities below, and list beside them what you can do for each person.

7. Are you ready to say the prayer of Ignatius of Loyola? Read it aloud now.

> Teach us, good Lord, to serve Thee as Thou deservest;
> To give and not to count the cost;
> To fight and not to heed the wounds;
> To toil and not to seek for rest;
> To labor and not to ask for any reward
> Save that of knowing that we do Thy will.

ANSWERS TO QUESTIONS

Question 2: Instead of comforting Job, they brought condemnation and the accusation we still hear today: "God is punishing you for your sins." For more about the friends' response, turn to pages 171–172.

Question 4: Compassion is showing pity, mercy, sympathy, kindliness, and concern, according to a synonym finder. Job put it this way: "I would speak in such a way that it would help you." Job was saying, "If I were your friend, I would cry with you, hug you, or hold you." He would show us God's love and help us through the grieving process.

FACILITATOR SUGGESTIONS

If you are using the video, go to Session 4 and begin with Sheila telling about Eleanor's last hour ("I saw that happening to my dear mother-in-law . . .") and play through to the end.

ASSIGNMENT FOR NEXT SESSION:
Read Chapter 12.

SESSION 12

TURNING POINT
When our dreams seem to go sour or remain unfulfilled, hopelessness can dominate our lives—or we can hold on with open hands, knowing that we have hope because God is faithful.

CHAPTER 12:
THERE IS A BETTER SONG TO SING

Introduction: The movie Steel Magnolias *is based on the true story of Pat Robinson and his wife, Susan. Pat decided that Susan's illness was a test from God, and he was not going to fail. He believed God was going to dramatically heal his wife as a testimony to all around her. But Susan was not healed. Even at her funeral Pat could not believe that God had not heard his prayer.*

In his loneliness he read the Bible, and as he kept his mind on God's Word and the promises he read there, peace began to edge out his despair. He read, "You will keep him

in perfect peace, / Whose mind is stayed on You" (Isaiah
26:3, NKJV).

1. What does perfect peace mean to you?

2. What is the biblical definition of peace in Isaiah 26:3?

3. What is the meaning of the phrase *whose mind is stayed
on You?*

4. Even though we would not choose suffering, it changes
our _____ of life and our _____ of God.

5. What is Job's condition at the end of the book of Job?
   Spiritually?

   Materially?

6. The story of Job is about a man who has seen the
_____.

ANSWERS TO QUESTIONS

Question 2: Perfect peace is translated from the Hebrew *shalom shalom*, which signifies fulfillment, abundance, well-being, security.

Question 3: The phrase *whose mind is stayed on You* comes from two Hebrew words: the first meaning "will, imagination"; the second, "dependent, supported, firm." When our wills and imaginations are dependent on God, when we choose to turn our thoughts to Him, we can find the simple truth that God is enough.

Question 4: Even though we would not choose suffering, it changes our <u>vision</u> of life and our <u>knowledge</u> of God.

Question 5: Spiritually—Job has completely surrendered to God and lives in peace. He has seen God and knows Him more intimately.

Materially—Job now has fourteen thousand sheep, six thousand camels, one thousand yoke of oxen, and one thousand female donkeys; twice what he had in the beginning. He also has seven sons and three daughters, the same number as in the beginning, but the first seven sons and three daughters are with God in heaven, so the number of his children has also doubled.

Question 6: The story of Job is about a man who has seen the <u>glory of the Lord.</u>

ASSIGNMENT FOR NEXT SESSION:
Read Chapter 13.

SESSION 13

TURNING POINT

When we face our choices, large or small, we can settle for lukewarm, diluted faith—or we can seek the real thing, because we know that one life does make a difference now and through all eternity.

CHAPTER 13:
ONE LIFE DOES MAKE A DIFFERENCE

*I*ntroduction: *Most of us would think that Ruth Glass, the beautiful wife of the CEO of Wal-Mart, had everything. Money. Prestige. A lovely home. Children. But Ruth became an alcoholic after she overcame her addiction to diet pills.*

Finally, after considering suicide, Ruth cried out to God to save her. And she began sitting down with her Bible— with a glass of wine and a cigarette—to read and reread the Gospels. One day she noticed that after she had been there for hours, the wineglass was still full. God had healed her heart. She didn't need alcohol anymore.

1. Do you think that Ruth's struggle, and yours, parallels Job's? _____ How?

2. Philip Yancey wrote, "The opening and closing . . . chapters of Job prove that God was greatly affected by the response of one man and that cosmic issues were at stake." He went on to say that the "wager" between God and Satan "resolved decisively that the faith of a single human being counts for very much, indeed."

Do you believe that this is true in your life? _____

3. How have you, like Job, withstood Satan's assault?

4. How can you do so in the future?

5. Do you sometimes feel as if God could be clapping for you? _____ If so, when?

6. Finally, think about the following Scripture:

What then shall we say to these things? If God is for us, who can be against us?

He who did not spare His own Son, but delivered Him up for us all, how shall He not with Him also freely give us all things?

Who shall bring a charge against God's elect? It is God who justifies.

Who is he who condemns? It is Christ who died, and furthermore is also risen, who is even at the right hand of God, who also makes intercession for us.

Who shall separate us from the love of Christ? Shall tribulation, or distress, or persecution, or famine, or nakedness, or peril, or sword?

As it is written:

> *"For Your sake we are killed*
> *all day long;*
> *We are accounted as sheep*
> *for the slaughter."*

Yet in all these things we are more than conquerors through Him who loved us.

For I am persuaded that neither death nor life, nor angels nor principalities nor powers, nor things present nor things to come, nor height nor depth, nor any other created thing, shall be able to separate us from the love of God which is in Christ Jesus our Lord.

Romans 8:31–39

AND REMEMBER . . .
LIFE IS TOUGH,
BUT GOD IS FAITHFUL.

ANSWERS TO QUESTIONS

Question 5: Be clear that God is clapping for you when you spend time with Him as well as when you are serving Him by your actions.

FACILITATOR SUGGESTIONS

This session is intended to be short so that it can be partly a celebration and social time. You might want to have refreshments or a luncheon and end this session by playing the song "God Is Faithful" from the *Hope* album.